THE
CLOUD
CHASER

Michael C. Watson, M.D.

THE CLOUD CHASER

A Physician's Early Adventures

Edited by Caroline N. Watson

TATE PUBLISHING
AND ENTERPRISES, LLC

Published by Tate Publishing & Enterprises, LLC
127 E. Trade Center Terrace | Mustang, Oklahoma 73064 USA
1.888.361.9473 | www.tatepublishing.com

Tate Publishing is committed to excellence in the publishing industry. The company reflects the philosophy established by the founders, based on Psalm 68:11,
"The Lord gave the word and great was the company of those who published it."

Book design copyright © 2014 by Tate Publishing, LLC. All rights reserved.
Cover design by Jim Villaflores
Interior design by Caypeeline Casas

Published in the United States of America

ISBN: 978-1-62902-972-6
1. Biography & Autobiography / Medical
2. Biography & Autobiography / Military
13.12.12

DEDICATION

This book is dedicated to my loving wife, Mary Carolyn, and longtime friend and associate, Marion Dwight, M.D. Without their encouragement and support, the events recorded in this book could not have been accomplished.

CONTENTS

Mickey at 3 years old

FAMILY AND CHILDHOOD

I was born on January 15, 1926, in my family's house on our farm near Ridge Spring, South Carolina. It was a sleepy town with a population of 550. Everyone knew everyone else and many families were related, as they had lived there for several generations. Like many Southerners of my age, my childhood was a rural one.

Ridge Spring lies in probably the richest farmland in the state—the ridge section, a long narrow region on the fall line, which marks the boundary between the foothills and the sand hills. When I left Ridge Spring as a young man and moved to Bamberg, a small town in South Carolina's sandy low country, an old admonition rang in my ears: "Never move off a good land."

If I hadn't left that good land, though, most of my story would have been very different from the one I am about to tell.

Mickey between Pat (left) and
Elizabeth (right) with Joe (back)

My parents had four children: Elizabeth, my big sister, was seven years older than me. Next came Mary Aurelia, usually called Patsy or Pat, who was two years younger than Elizabeth. Then two years later came Joseph Watson III, my brother Joe, who was three years older. I was named after my mother's father, Michael Cunningham. However, Father insisted that nobody calls me Mike, as he had a relative, a Mike Watson, who was not an admirable man in Father's eyes. He was not a good farmer and had lost his land. Furthermore, he had an alcohol problem. Therefore, Father did not wish me to share that name. So until I left home for college, nobody called me Mike. Almost everyone called me Mickey. Most of my boyhood friends still call me Mickey, but anyone who has met me as an adult calls me Mike. Mama usually called me Michael, as did my sisters. Father always called me Mickey or Mickey-man.

Elizabeth, my oldest sister, always looked out for me. And I think that when I came along, Mama was very busy, and Elizabeth accepted and liked the idea of taking care of the baby in the family. To this day, she and I have a special relationship. The two middle children, Pat and Joe, also shared a special relationship. And Joe, being my older brother, was always an idol and mentor to me.

Family of Joseph Calhoun Watson (on father's knee)

Father: Joseph Calhoun Watson

My father, Joseph Calhoun Watson, was born in the family home in Ridge Spring in 1887. My grandfather was also a Joseph, but my father was never known as junior, as his father died when he was only nine years old. From that time on, he had to be a man, for his own mother seemed to be a dependent sort of person who needed other people to make decisions for her. She had broken her leg at a fairly young age and never fully recovered. In a sense, my father never had a childhood, for even though he had an uncle who helped out, my father essentially ran the family place.

When I say that my father ran the family place, I don't mean that he did the manual labor himself. My father was gentry, and in those days, Southern whites of a certain class did not do field work. Black people did that. Nevertheless, at a very young age, Father had to take on many adult management responsibilities.

My father's life was not always hard, and his family provided him with a sound education at Wofford College in Spartanburg, South Carolina. In high school, he was quite a baseball pitcher. When he arrived at Wofford, around 1907, he went out for the school's baseball team. But the coach told him that the team already had enough pitchers. What they needed was a first baseman, so Father said he'd give first base a try, and he made the team. But after a while, he stopped going to practices. When the coach came to his room to ask him about it, Father told him that first base just didn't appeal to him. So Father was dropped from the team, which was about to go on tour. In those days, schools and towns all had their own teams, and those teams would travel by train from place to place, playing other local teams. To get ready for its tour, Wofford College scheduled a game with the local Spartanburg city team.

Well, when Father played in high school, his team had traveled to Spartanburg and played with the city's team. Ridge Spring was a tiny hamlet and Spartanburg was a city of many thousands. But Father had pitched, and Ridge Spring had won the game. When the Spartanburg team learned that Father was not playing for Wofford, they asked him to pitch for them against the college team. He pitched a no-hitter. The next day, when the college team boarded the train to go on tour, Father boarded with them—as their pitcher. This was the time of Ty Cobb, Christy Matthewson, and Honus Wagner.

He had quite a career on the Wofford baseball team and got several offers to play professional baseball. But even if he had been interested in professional baseball as a career, he was never offered any significant money, so he stayed in school, graduated, and went back home to continue running the family farm.

Joseph Calhoun Watson as Wofford College pitcher

Uncle Roy

Father had a younger brother named Leroy, better known to us as Uncle Roy. He was a happy-go-lucky young man, whereas my father was a more steady and dependable sort. When the United States entered World War I, Uncle Roy was called up. Father was also of age to serve, but he was deferred because he ran the farm. While Uncle Roy was stationed at Camp Taylor near Greer, South Carolina, he contracted influenza in the pandemic of 1918–1919. As a complication of this, he then developed pneumonia and emphysema, which is an infection in the chest cavity. It had to be drained over a course of many months, and during that time, Roy started drinking heavily. I recall Mama saying that in the long months of hospitalization, he received plenty of money from home, and his comrades encouraged him to spend it on alcohol. (This may have been the family's rationalization of the situation.) Eventually, Uncle Roy became an alcoholic; and despite several admissions to inpatient facilities for prolonged treatment, he remained an alcoholic for the rest of his life. He died in 1925 at the age of thirty-three.

When I was growing up, both of my parents were adamantly opposed to the drinking of alcohol. No alcoholic beverage of any kind, even for cooking, was allowed in our house. I imagine that Uncle Roy's alcoholism played a big role in their attitude.

Aurelia Cunningham (right) at Winthrop College

Mama: Mamie Aurelia Cunningham

It was during the years preceding World War I that my mother moved to Ridge Spring to work as a teacher in our school.

My mother's name was Mamie Aurelia Cunningham, but she didn't like the name Mamie; she went by Aurelia. The Cunninghams were an old Southern family who first came to America in the 1600s and settled in Virginia. A relative of my mother, Anne Pamela Cunningham, was influential in saving Mount Vernon as a national historic site before the Civil War. My mother's grandfather graduated from Washington College in Lexington, Virginia (now Washington and Lee University), and after graduate studies at the University of Virginia moved to Mississippi. He then moved to Reidsville, South Carolina, where he was the headmaster of a school. Reidsville is just south of Greer, South Carolina, and after a time, he moved his family to Greer.

My mother was born on January 6, 1894, in Greer, which is upstate South Carolina in the foothills of the mountains. She graduated from Winthrop College (now Winthrop University) in Rock Hill, South Carolina. It was a special thing back then for a woman to earn a college degree, but she came from a family that valued education; and her father, despite the fact that he had eight children (all but one of whom were girls), saw that all of them had the opportunity to attend college. Everyone earned a college degree, except the youngest who graduated from a business school.

As children, we all loved to look at Mama's Winthrop annual and see Miss Aurelia Cunningham with a group of laughing young girls wearing white long-sleeved blouses and ankle length skirts with their hair pinned up on top of their heads.

Aurelia Cunningham (center) at Winthrop

Family History and Family Legends

Before my parents ever met, there was a connection between the Watsons and the Cunninghams. It seems that there was once in South Carolina a William "Bloody Bill" Cunningham, a Tory leader during the Revolutionary War who was notorious for his cruelty. And in Ridge Spring, there lived a Michael Watson, who was a captain in the Revolutionary Army. I have heard that Bloody Bill's troops once chased Michael Watson across the Saluda River. My sister Elizabeth remembers hearing a story that Michael Watson and Bloody Bill Cunningham once fought a duel. My brother, Joe, says that as he understands it, Michael Watson and Bloody Bill Cunningham never met, but Watson was, in fact, killed by Cunningham's men.

It is always difficult to know the exact truth of such old stories, but both sides of my family are related in one degree or another to these two participants in the Revolutionary War. I suppose you could say that my parents' marriage finally ended whatever bad blood existed between the Watsons and the Cunninghams.

Aurelia Cunningham Watson with Mickey's sister Elizabeth

Aurelia and Cal Marry

While my mother was teaching in Ridge Spring, she met both my father and my uncle Roy. As I understand it, she dated Uncle Roy first but at some point began seeing my father instead. My father used to say that he had long believed that he would never marry but would instead remain a bachelor and spend his days caring for his mother and tending the family land. He assumed that it would be Uncle Roy who would carry on the family name. But then Aurelia entered his life, and all his plans were changed. In 1917, my father proposed marriage, but my mother did not accept it immediately. In fact, she moved back to Greer to consider what course her life should take, and she stayed there for a year. During that year, my father visited her on several occasions. He used to tell her about the hot train ride from Ridge Spring to Greer and how he kept "those little girls" (her sisters) busy bringing him water to drink after his arrival at the family home in Greer.

Mama finally accepted Father's proposal and on August 29, 1918, they were married at the home of her Aunt Mamie Walker, her father's sister, in Greenville, South Carolina.

At the time they married, Father was still living with and caring for his mother, so Mama moved into the family home. She was too much of a lady to complain openly about living with her mother-in-law, who, apparently, was not an easy person to get along with, but Mama didn't much like it from what I gathered. My sister Pat remembers hearing that one day, Father was sitting on the front porch, talking with his mother, when he heard Mama turn on the Victrola and play "I'll Take You Home Again, Kathleen," the story of an Irish bride who was lonely and homesick. To Father's credit, he realized that Mama too was feeling lonely and homesick and took her for a buggy ride.

In 1921, they moved into the house that Father built for her, a house of her own. It was a large, red brick house, which my parents named but hardly ever called *Alhambra*, the Arabic term for "the red house." This is the house where I was born in 1926.

Mickey's boyhood home, built by his father and named *Alhambra*

The Grove

The farm itself—about 100 acres—had largely been in the Watson family since before the Revolutionary War. It was a portion of the land that had been deeded to the family at various times by Kings George II and George III of England. We had another piece of land that was not contiguous, which we referred to simply as "the other place." Besides the house—which you approach on a semicircular driveway with entrances that passed between two brick columns—we had a well and pump house, a billy goat shed, a two-story cow barn and three-story mule barn, a cotton house, an asparagus packing house, a scales shed with scales that could weigh wagons and later trucks along with their loads, two chicken houses, a smokehouse where we salt-cured the meat from the pigs that were butchered, a blacksmith shop, two tenant houses, and a two-car garage made of red brick to match the house. All of this was located in a grove of oak trees, which is why everyone called this part of the property The Grove. My brother Joe still owns most of the farmland, but we sold The Grove and Alhambra after Mama died.

The house was designed in traditional Georgian architecture. It was a three-story house with a wide masonry porch and large white columns that supported the two-story roof over the front porch. On the second story, overlooking the porch was a small balcony. At the time my father built it, the house was considered quite modern. For one thing, the kitchen was actually in the house, which was different from many houses built before then. Usually, the kitchens were built separately out in the backyard. In this way, the living quarters could escape the heat generated by cooking. There was a button used to ring a bell in the butler's pantry, in the floor by the hostess's seat at the dining room table. The butler's pantry was a room between the dining room and the kitchen. I don't remember that we ever actually had a butler, but that was the way the house was built.

The large porch was a wonderful place to sit on hot days, and sometimes some of us would sleep out there on hot nights. After our naps in the afternoon, we would often sit on the porch drinking blackberry acid, a drink that Mama made. We had a large blackberry patch in our backyard, and she used its berries to make a kind of concentrate. To prepare the drink, she would pour a small amount of the concentrate in a glass, add sugar, fill it with water, and a lump of ice. The ice was chipped off the larger piece that stayed in the icebox to cool milk and other things that are now kept in refrigerators.

Mickey with his father and sisters on
front porch of boyhood home

My father valued self-reliance above almost any other thing, and he liked the idea that he was lord of his domain and that everything that was in his domain came from his land. It gave him great pleasure to sit down to a meal and eat meat from animals that he had raised and butchered, bread from wheat that he had harvested and milled, and vegetables that he had planted. So it went along with my father's character that all the timber put into the house was taken from the farm itself. And all the timber was heart pine. He would get a charge out of pest control people who would want to check for termites. He'd tell them to go right ahead and check, but, of course, they never found anything, as termites can't tolerate heart pine.

The house had twelve-foot ceilings, making it very open and airy. As you entered through the front door, you came into a large hall with French doors on either side. On the left side, you would enter the sitting room, where guests would sit. On the other side of the hall was the family room although we didn't call it that. We called it the nursery. Off the sitting room was a large dining room, and off that was a glassed-in sun porch where Mama kept all her plants in the wintertime. There were doors onto the sun porch from both the sitting room and the dining room. Across the hall from the dining room, there was also a downstairs bedroom that was called Mama's room. From this room, she supervised our baths in the adjacent bathroom, read us Bible stories, asked each of us to talk about something good that we had done for someone that day, and heard our prayers every night as we knelt at her knee. This established a lifelong habit for me, and I still kneel by my bed to pray every night.

Off the nursery, there was a porte-cochere, a covered passageway outside the house that balanced the sun porch on the opposite side. When people came to visit, the driver would stop the car there, let the passengers out so they could enter the house through the nursery, and then drive on to the parking area at the back.

The entry hall was long and perhaps twelve feet wide with a stairway running up the left-hand wall. It then crossed to the right, turned again, and ended at the upstairs hallway. The downstairs hall continued into the butler's pantry and kitchen, and beyond that was a big screened-in back porch.

The stairs were wide and handsome, and one of Mama's dearest wishes was to have her daughters get married in the house and walk down those stairs in their wedding gowns, which is exactly what my oldest sister Elizabeth did. Pat, however, got married in New York, as her fiancé was stationed there and couldn't leave. According to Elizabeth, that was just as well. She told me recently that she had never wanted to walk down those stairs in a wedding gown as she knew it would be a nightmare to get through, and it was. But she didn't want to disappoint Mama.

Behind the house, to the right of the screened porch, was a big, circular, brick-encased, open well though it had a wooden cover across the opening. This well house had a pump room behind it, and both were covered with a slate roof. This structure was connected to the screened porch by a short concrete ramp. We could draw water up with a bucket, but as soon as electricity became available in the area, an electric pump was installed. After that, water was not drawn with buckets for general household use.

The water came from a bed of blue clay, and Father continued to drink water drawn with the bucket for some years, as he liked the taste better. Years later, the town extended the municipal waterworks as far as the road in front of our house. Father ran a pipe from our house and connected it to Ridge Spring's water system. When the plumbing work was completed, he turned on the spigot and drank a glass of city water. Then he closed the connection, and we continued to drink well water. He didn't like the taste of city water.

Mickey behind his sister Pat and brother Joe
on a mule in front of *Alhambra*

A Mule-Powered Farm

Those were the days of non-mechanized agriculture when the work on our farm was done by mule power. I know that adventuresome little boys can find many things of interest on a farm in these mechanized times, but I don't think anything approaches the attraction of mules and wagons and sleds. Sleds were crude wooden platforms with two runners on the bottom. These were pulled behind a mule in the furrows between rows of asparagus. The interesting thing for me about this means of transportation was there was absolutely no coasting. The stops were extremely abrupt, and any unwary rider could easily be thrown forward and often to the ground, which made it all the more fun.

One area around the farm held a special fascination for me and that was the blacksmith shop. My father maintained the blacksmith shop even though Mr. Padgett, the blacksmith, had a shop of his own about three miles away. Nonetheless, Father would have Mr. Padgett come by and use our shop to fit the mules with shoes and shrink the iron tires to the wagon wheels as well as other things. I am sure Father had that blacksmith shop mainly to reinforce his feeling of self-reliance. I used to love to go out and watch Mr. Padgett heat up a horseshoe to red hot, shape it, and plunge it into the cold water to temper it. As a little boy, that was an exciting moment, hearing the sizzle of water against hot metal and watching all the steam come up. Once the shoe was cooled, he would nail it to the mule's hoof.

Nowadays, when you join metal, you weld the two pieces with a torch. But in those days, you would heat both pieces of metal that you were going to weld and then pound them, then heat them again, then pound them again until finally they'd be melded completely. When I was at Clemson, all the electrical engineering students had to take forge and foundry, which includes what a blacksmith does, and I remember doing that work as a college student and thinking back on my childhood.

Later on, it cost too much to have Mr. Padgett come out to our place, as farming became more mechanized. There were fewer and fewer mules, so I would take jobs to his shop; and even though I was older, I still enjoyed watching him do his work.

Mickey, his brother and sister in a mule-drawn
wagon driven by one of the hands

The Hands

I loved to ride in the mule-drawn wagons with the hands, the black laborers who worked on the farm. From age five and up, I would sometimes be away from home for hours at a time. As well as I can remember, my parents didn't worry about me at all—a little white boy being cared for by one or more black men. My parents knew these people, and their trust in them was complete. They were always kind, gentle, and generous, and I loved them. In fact, the early exposure I had to these wonderful people shaped my feelings about black people for the rest of my life.

During the unrest in the '60s, I had to sort out my feelings about the race situation. I found that many people were afraid of black people or even hated them simply because they were black. Both of these feelings were diametrically opposed to my feelings, even though I too was "prejudiced." What do I mean by that? I came to understand that being "prejudiced" meant that it was acceptable for whites and blacks to interact with each other as long as the black people stayed "in their place." American society was highly segregated from the time I was a child until I was an adult, and that was just the way it was in those days. The white people who lived in the South had not created racial prejudice, but we did perpetuate it. I suppose that keeping things as they always have been offers people a certain sense of security.

As I puzzled over this situation as an adult, I realized that Southerners had a different struggle to face than the rest of the nation that didn't have a close relationship with black people. The prejudices that Southerners had to change about their perception of black people were different from the ones that people from other regions had to change. All we had to do was recognize that "their place" was not what we had forced on them for so long but the place of equals in every sense. I feel that this is the primary reason that the South had an easier time being "desegregated" than many other areas of our country.

Hauling Sugar Cane for Grinding

In my childhood, though, none of these complicated concerns troubled me. I simply accepted the way things were and enjoyed the life of a Southern farm boy.

One of my most vivid recollections is of getting up early one fall morning when I was about five years old, climbing with two of the hands onto a wagon loaded with sugarcane, and riding to the cane mill, a distance of about five or six miles. I still remember how exciting it was to ride through the town early in the morning on a wagon pulled by two mules. After leaving town, we rode again past fields and woods until we came to the mill where the cane grinding began. The "mill" was actually no more than a simple contraption involving two vertical rollers between which the stalks of cane were fed and crushed. The operation was powered by a mule, walking around in a circle under a "boom," which transmitted the power to the rollers.

The cane juice ran down from the rollers, collected in buckets, and was taken to the "cooker," a large pan with a wood fire beneath it. The temperature was carefully controlled to avoid burning the syrup while still allowing the evaporation process to proceed as rapidly as possible.

This process took all day long—an interminable time for a small boy. I remember how the day dragged. I had brought a lunch from home—two biscuits and a baked sweet potato. About noontime, I got out my lunch, and the mill operator saw it and said, "You want some zip, boy?" I agreed a little hesitantly, as I wasn't sure what "zip" was. Then, he poured a generous amount of fresh and delicious tasting syrup on my biscuits.

By the end of the day, all the cane had been ground, and the juice had been cooked long enough to turn into thick syrup, which was poured into tin buckets. Then, the three of us climbed back onto the wagon and made the long trip home, arriving after dark.

The one bad thing that I learned from the hands was something that was not done in a mean or spiteful way but in the spirit of fun. Nevertheless, it had far-reaching consequences for me.

I don't recall how it started, but the hands began to goad me into fighting any little black boy that we encountered. This continued for several years and all of us thought it was great fun. I don't recall anyone getting hurt. From that beginning, though, I became more and more easily upset and quick to lose my temper. I remember when I was in seventh grade, another boy did something to me that I considered offensive. I became so angry that I vomited. My mother saw this exhibition and said something that changed my life. She said, "If you don't learn to control yourself, you'll never control anyone else."

I thought about this for many years. I had to learn to control myself. I realized that anger is a destructive emotion and deprives the angry person of the ability to reason or control himself, much less others, except through fear. So I worked on this almost constantly for years. Now I don't have to. Anger is not an option in my life anymore. I recall at a meeting of the medical staff years ago, I was saying something, and one of the other physicians said, heatedly, "That's a damn lie." I didn't pause or respond in any way to what he had said, and I think he became ashamed. One of the others came up to me after the meeting and said, "I've never seen anyone like you before. You didn't pay any attention to him at all."

Clouds Creek and Other Summer Places

More often than not, I tend to recollect my early childhood as a progression of long summer days. And many of those summer days were spent at Clouds Creek, which was a slow, meandering stream about three miles behind our house. Elizabeth says that Clouds Creek is one of the boundaries mentioned in one of our original land grants. When I was very young, aged five to eight, Joe would take me there, and sometimes we'd be joined by his friend, Wallace Steadman, Jr. Later on, I would go with my own friends. Bruce Timmerman and Brice Jordan were especially good friends in those early days. We used to walk there almost every summer day. The creek had some deep holes where we could swim, and it was spanned by a wooden bridge from which we did most of our fishing. In my memory, Clouds Creek has always filled an enormous space, but I remember going by the creek after I had been away a number of years and being surprised and disappointed by how small it actually seemed.

At Clouds Creek as an adult with
daughter Caroline

As I reminisce about those expeditions to Clouds Creek, I tend to picture the world as being carefree and benign. However, my sister Pat later told me that Mama didn't see those boyhood journeys as entirely safe. She remembers Mama telling her that she always had this fearful image in her head of two little bodies floating down that stream. I suppose, though, that Mama knew we needed our independence.

She also went out of her way to make time for us. I remember that when I was a very young child, she would take the four of us and our dog Prince and walk to a spot we called The Little Camp, some distance behind the house. There we would have a picnic and sometimes build a fire to cook hot dogs and toast marshmallows on sticks.

Another favorite picnic place was The Old Shoals. This was a smooth rock formation over which a creek flowed and spilled into a basin at the bottom. It was great fun to slide down the slick slope of the shoals and into the basin. We all put on shorts and sometimes wore holes in the seats. We usually went with the Steadman family, who had four children in our age group. Mr. and Mrs. Wallace Steadman were probably my parents' closest friends. Mr. Steadman was a farmer and the superintendent of the local school district. Wallace Jr. was one of Joe's best friends, and Patty Steadman became my boyhood sweetheart.

Sometimes Elizabeth, Pat, Joe, and I would stay overnight with the Steadman family. The highlight of such a stay would always be the stories Mrs. Steadman told about the "time when she was a man." These were fabulous stories of adventures that only a man could have. All eight of the children would be absolutely entranced.

Chasing a Cloud and Other Adventures

As a boy, I thought my brother Joe knew everything. I remember asking him all kinds of questions. And his answers to me were always the gospel.

I remember one hot summer day walking with Joe to Clouds Creek. As we strolled along the familiar dirt road to the creek, I saw—just ahead of us and moving in the same direction—the huge shadow of a cloud.

I remarked to Joe, "If we hurry up and run and catch up to that shadow, we will be able to walk in its shade."

Joe just snorted. "You can't catch a cloud," he said.

I remember saying under my breath, "I think I can," as I bolted ahead, caught, and breathlessly walked in the shade of the cloud.

I never forgot that day nor the lesson that "to catch a cloud, you first have to chase it."

From then on, even though I still respected Joe, I started to realize that maybe he didn't know everything. He was a good older brother, though, and he always looked out for me. He did, however, think that I was lazy. I didn't like farm work, and he did. He couldn't figure out what could be wrong with me except that I must be lazy.

When I was five or six years old, the summer uniform for Southern country boys was short trousers and a belt to hold the trousers up. Very simple—no shoes, no socks, no shirts. As boys like to do, we loved to explore the woods behind our house. One day, Joe, Wallace Steadman Jr., and I were exploring the woods. We decided that we would collect some dead wood that was lying around and take it home to use. The fact that we had a wood-house full of wood did not enter our minds.

As we began to collect the wood, it became obvious that we could carry only a few pieces in our hands, so we took off our belts to bundle the wood. This, however, led to a problem—our trousers fell down around our ankles. Very quickly, though, a solution appeared—a number of sturdy vines that grew in the area. So we used our belts to carry the wood and made suspenders from some of the vines, and that did the trick.

By next morning, though, we had all broken out with an itching rash that rapidly spread over our bodies; it became obvious that the nice vines we had used were poison ivy. Pretty soon we were all bedridden, and though I never saw the others, I was told that my rash was the worst of the three. I was literally covered from head to toe. My fingers were so swollen that the spaces between my fingers were obliterated, and my hands were fan-shaped. I can remember making a fist and fluid poured out of ruptured blebs as my fingers came together. Both of my eyes were badly swollen: one was completely shut and the other provided me with only a slit of vision. A thick crust formed over my eyelid margins.

The itching was excruciating all over! But I was repeatedly cautioned not to scratch, as this would only make it worse. I did as I was told, although the urge to scratch was intense, and so I have no scars on my skin from that experience. The poison ivy took ten days to subside, ten endless days when you are a six-year-old confined to bed. When at last the symptoms began to resolve, the thick crust that had formed over my eyelid margins came off, and I could see again although my eyelashes came out with the crust. Fortunately, they grew back.

That experience taught me patience and the ability to ignore irritants of all kinds. It also taught me to recognize poison ivy plants at thirty feet!

We used to cut sticks with our pocketknives and fish down at Clouds Creek. My father always insisted that each of his sons carry a small pocketknife. I suspect this was a holdover from the days when people used knives to sharpen the tips of their quill pens and, later, pencils. None of my boys ever expressed any interest in carrying a pocketknife, but as I find them very useful, I asked one of them why he didn't want one.

"Daddy," he told me, "I'd get expelled from school if I carried one of those."

Times change.

I remember once that I had lost mine and got a severe scolding—and a new knife. From then on, I always had a sharp pocketknife in my pocket, and to this day, still carry a small penknife. In fact, a pocketknife once played a role in a dramatic situation I faced during my internship after medical school. But I won't get into that here.

One of my memories of Father and his pocketknife is of walks we would sometimes take with him. He loved to walk around his farm after work, and we used to enjoy stepping in his tracks as we followed him through freshly plowed fields. During sugarcane harvest season, he often took along a long stalk of sugarcane. He would take out his pocketknife and cut out a section of the cane, peel it, cut it longways, and give each of us a section to chew. It was sweet and so juicy that the juice would run down your chin!

We planted only a few rows of sugarcane, and I suspect that this was planted primarily for us to have syrup on our table from our own cane. Father loved syrup, which he poured on hot buttered biscuits from the silver syrup pitcher with his initials on it.

Camping with the Family

As Mama had grown up in Greer, she had a special affection for the mountains, and we used to vacation there every summer. Some of my earliest and best memories are of camping trips to the Pisgah Forest campgrounds in western North Carolina. Father would borrow a large tent and we would head off as a small caravan, the family in our Ford Model A and a black man and a black woman in a truck behind us. The man pitched the tent, helped to unpack, and tended the fire while the woman cooked and made wonderful meals. I don't remember but one or two such expeditions, and then the Depression came, and that ended those trips.

When we could no longer afford that kind of vacation, my uncle's brother-in-law would allow us to use his mountain house at Caesar's Head, so Mama still was able to be in her beloved mountains for one week each summer. Later on, we rented a cabin in Oconee State Park near Walhalla and spent a week there each summer.

Pat says that Father taking Mama camping each summer was a true testimony to his devotion to her, as he was no camper. He liked things clean and pressed and no bugs.

He was a compulsive hand-washer, and so am I; it must be the genes. On more than one occasion, I observed how he would shake hands with someone and then not put his right hand in his pocket again until after he had washed it. He had a separate towel at the sink where he washed his hands when he came in from outside. I can sympathize, as I too have learned how grimy little hands can make a towel. Fortunately, my compulsion about hand washing has fit right into my professional life as a physician. During my years in medical school and active practice, as proper hand washing became emphasized more and more, I was held up as a model for hand washing.

Mickey's mother enjoying an annual camping trip

Mickey in every day (except Sunday) summer attire

THE DEPRESSION YEARS

As for most Americans, the Great Depression changed life radically for my family. Before the Depression, we would have been considered to be at least upper middle class, but afterwards we were very poor, as so many other families were.

At the time my mother and father were first married, the farm was planted mainly in cotton, and cotton was still king in the South back then. But the Depression came along and cotton went down to a nickel a pound. Then the boll weevil appeared and killed the cotton production. My father used to tell a joke about getting rid of boll weevils. He had a wonderful sense of humor, and I remember how he laughed when he told this story. It seems that *The Farmer's Bulletin* came out with an ad from a man that said, "Send me $2.00, and I will send you back a sure-fire cure that will kill boll weevils." So folks sent in their $2.00, and the man sent back his sure-fire cure. He said, "Take a boll weevil and put it on a block of wood. Then hit it with another block of wood. That's a sure-fire cure for the boll weevil." My father thought that was the funniest thing.

Unfortunately, with the collapse of the cotton market and the beginning of the Depression, the farm couldn't bring in enough cash to pay the bills, so my father took a job with one of the local banks. I remember how he used to take me with him, and he would write me a check for a nickel. I would take the check into the bank and give it to the teller who would hand me back a nickel, which my father would let me use to buy whatever I wanted.

Father Assigned to Kentucky

As the Depression went on, though, things got tougher still. Banks closed; everything was depressed. I wasn't old enough to know the particulars, but I knew that these were bad times. With the banks closing, my father lost his job. Fortunately, he found another one with the Seed Loan, which was a part of the Department of Agriculture during the New Deal. This agency provided farmers with low interest loans to help them plant their crops. Not long after he started, the agency asked him to take a temporary transfer to Kentucky. He was a strong family man, but this was in the depths of the Depression, and I am sure that he was grateful to have any job at all, as people were desperately poor. So he took the job with the idea that it would last three months.

It lasted seven years, from 1933 until 1940. He left when I was seven and returned when I was fourteen. Of course, he wasn't gone the entire time. He came home for a week each summer and another week at Christmas. And he always wrote, telling Mama what she needed to do regarding the farm. Since my father was officially on a temporary assignment in Kentucky, he was paid per diem for his meals and mileage and for the accommodations where he lived, so that was a real good job in those days. He lived very frugally and poured his earnings back into the farm. Something else he did that tells me a lot about him was that throughout the entire time he was away, he collected all the Sunday comics and mailed them back to us.

Mama and Bennie Raiford Take Charge

Though he gave her all the advice he could, it was up to Mama to manage the place. My mother grew up living in town and didn't know a thing about agriculture. Once my father left for Kentucky, though, she became the manager of a large farming operation that employed between five and ten black men who came to her for answers to all their questions. Father made the major decisions, but making sure everything got done was up to her. I don't know how she managed. She was a very strong and capable person.

The savior in this situation was a very large and gentle black man named Bennie Raiford. He acted as foreman and, I imagine, was the *sine qua non* of the situation. Bennie was a big part of my childhood and the image of his giant figure always looms large in memory.

Joseph Calhoun Watson

Father's Character

Another giant though distant figure during those years of the Depression was my father. To me he was almost mythical, probably because he was more spoken of than seen, and we all looked forward to whatever time he could spend at home. As we were preparing for one of his summer visits, I remember drawing some laughter when I asked Mama, "We will have to wear shoes when Father is here, won't we?" This was the ultimate in deference, as I wore shoes only to church in those days.

Father was a reserved, almost an austere person, at least on first meeting, although he could be warm and friendly once he got to know a person. Part of that behavior probably came from his own character and the demanding circumstances of his childhood, but another part surely came from the social manners of the day. Men and women of his generation were very formal, much more so than people of my generation. In my entire life, I seldom saw him in anything other than a suit (seersucker in the summertime). I doubt that he even owned a sports shirt. And very few people called him by his first name. To close friends, he was Cal. To his four children, he was Father. To everyone else, he was Mr. Watson or Mr. Cal. My mother, on the other hand, was always referred to as Mama, which indicates the less formal relationship we had with her.

I remember my father largely as an older man. I was born when he was forty years of age, and he left home, except for two weeks each year when I was seven years old. He returned when I was fourteen, but for all practical purposes, the relationship was lost in the years in between. My two sisters and brother were old enough to have established a more complete relationship with him.

When I was about fifteen, an incident involving my father occurred that made an indelible impression on me.

I had ridden with him to Batesburg when a man backed his car into ours and put a long dent on the side. The man got out of his car, apologized, and told Father that if he would take his car around to the repair shop and get it fixed, he would pay the bill. So we took the car there, and Father pointed out the dent to the repairman. Actually, there were two dents, perfectly in line. The repairman assumed that both were the result of the accident, but Father was quick to point out that one was the result of a previous accident and that he would be responsible for that one.

All he had to do was stay quiet and no one would have known the difference, but he impressed me that day. That kind of honesty was uncompromising.

Father rarely, if ever, displayed emotion. He was almost detached from his family in that sense. I remember at Christmas, he would watch us open our presents, apparently enjoying our pleasure, but then he would get up and take his own presents into another room to open them by himself. He had lost his own paternal role model at a very young age, and I suspect he didn't know how to be emotionally close to his own children.

Because of my deep reverence for my father as my role model, I recognized early in my own marriage that I was very much like him. I look a lot like him, and I act a lot like him or so my brother, Joe, says. For instance, when my children give me my Christmas presents, I tend to just sit there and wait a long time before I finally open them. I think about him every time I do that. Nevertheless, I didn't want my children growing up feeling that their father was detached from them emotionally. So I made a conscious effort to be close and loving and went out of my way to say and do things that made them know that they were special.

Hard Times on the Farm

I don't remember all the hardships that my parents must have had to deal with during the Great Depression. I think Mama shielded us from the situation as much as she could. I do, however, remember two incidents that seemed pretty dramatic to me at the time.

The first occurred when someone told Mama that the sheriff had posted a sign at the end of our front drive, giving notice that the property was to be sold for failure to pay taxes. Like so many other folks back then, my folks couldn't keep up with the taxes, but Mama went right out to the big brick columns at the entrance of our drive and tore the sign down.

After this, Mama swallowed her pride and went to Uncle George Strother, whose family lived across the road, and told him about her problem. At this, she said that he reached into his pocket, took out his wallet, and removed several bills and gave them to her. Elizabeth says that she wept as she told her about this. That was the last we heard about selling the farm for taxes.

In a similar vein, I remember that the owner of the local telephone exchange called one day and requested payment on our account, which was past due. I didn't hear but one side of the conversation but I heard Mama say, "I intend to pay you when I can, but if you can't wait, just come and take the telephone out." He never came back.

Besides running the farm and raising four children, Mama also returned to teaching at the local school, the job that had originally brought her to Ridge Spring from college. Many times she was paid in "script," a promissory note that the schools had to use, as they often had no funds to pay the teachers. I remember on one occasion being at the grocery store with Mama when she had thirty-five cents to buy groceries for the week. We were lucky that we had to buy very few staples.

I know all that was hard on her, and I am surprised how painful it is to recollect and write about this particular phase of our lives, especially because of my empathy for Mama. This must have been a very trying time for her.

Effects of the Depression Today

I was very young during the worst years of the Depression and was not aware of any other way of life, so the very frugal way that we lived made an indelible impression on me.

One of the regular topics of conversation that I overheard was talk about life insurance. Paying utility bills, grocery bills, and taxes were all important, but the one thing that I understood for certain was that my parents had to make that life insurance payment. Everything was second to that. Everything was second to that payment so that if anything happened to Father, Mama, his children, and the farm could keep going. When he finally died in 1963, he still had that insurance policy. It was for $10,000. The way he and Mama had talked about it back in the thirties, you would have thought it was worth $150,000. Of course, back when he took it out, $10,000 was big money.

To this day, I have difficulty throwing anything away that might possibly be of use later on. I am addicted to bargains, and Mary Carolyn and I spend very frugally. In our early lives, we didn't have much money, and we have continued that behavior. I think many from our generation are like that. We typically took the attitude that if you didn't have it, you couldn't spend, so there was no use worrying about it.

Happiness in Hard Times

Because we were accustomed to such a frugal way of looking at the world, we didn't always see those times as so bad. I have many happy childhood memories despite the Depression. Life in a small town always had joys and adventures. Because we lived on a farm, we were better off than many, as we could raise many of our own staples. Father took great pride in that. We had flour ground from our wheat, grits and cornmeal ground from our corn, pork from our pigs, eggs and chickens from our yard, fruit from our pear, apple, and peach trees, and an abundance of vegetables from our garden. We also had a scuppernong arbor and blackberry vines.

And even during the Depression, a big day each year was the day we butchered a pig—cut it up, salted it down, put the meat in the smokehouse, and rendered the fat into lard and cracklings in a large iron pot over an open fire. The "hands" who lived in The Grove shared the work and the fresh meat. There was a holiday atmosphere on butchering day, and everyone had a good time.

There was also no end of trouble to be gotten into on a farm. And Joe and I were no less daring and adventuresome than other boys growing up in the country. A few adventures in particular come to mind, and I don't believe that my parents ever learned about them.

In addition to the well near the house, we had another large open well out near the barn. It had a chain that went down the well with a bucket on each end of the chain. If you drew one bucket, the other bucket went down. Once when I was about twelve years old (and it still makes me tremble to think of this), I dropped something into that well. I don't even remember what it was, but I do remember that I wanted it back; so I slid down the chain to get it, and I was soon standing in the water about twenty or thirty feet down. Right away, I realized that I was really cold, freezing, and taking deep, labored breaths. I didn't know what was going on, but I knew that I had better get out of there. So I climbed, hand over hand, back up that chain, and swung myself over the edge of the well. I felt very weak, but in a few minutes I was all right.

Later on, I read that the water in such wells flows through soil that contains high concentrations of calcium carbonate. Carbon dioxide is released into the water and then into the air and accumulates at the bottom of the well. Carbon dioxide is a heavy gas, far heavier than air. So my guess is that the carbon dioxide content of the air I had been breathing was very high, and the oxygen content was very low. Had I stayed down there much longer, I would have been unconscious in a matter of minutes. And since no one had seen me go down the well, no one would have known to help me. It scares me more now, looking back on it and realizing what sort of danger I was in, than it did at the time it occurred.

The next incident happened to Joe, rather than me, although I was involved.

We had two barns in The Grove. One was three stories and the other one was two stories, which had a gabled roof that came down at sharp angles. Joe and I loved to fill crocus sacks with leaves or straw, get up to the top, and slide down until we got to the place where it wasn't so steep. I remember one time we were doing that—sliding down the steep angle, coming to a stop where the angle of the roof changed, climbing back up the roof, and sliding down again. To get up on the roof, we had to walk across along a narrow board from the shed next to the roof. On one trip, Joe fell the entire two stories down to the barnyard. It didn't knock him out, but he was not himself and I didn't know what his injuries were. Fortunately, he returned to normal in a few minutes, and everything turned out to be fine. But we never told our parents. I never told anybody. In fact, I'm not sure I've ever told anybody about going into that well either.

I wouldn't say that Joe and I were daredevils, but I think we had a lot of confidence, maybe foolish confidence and maybe overconfidence at times. For example, when I was about fifteen, I went swimming with some friends in a pond between Batesburg and Leesville. It was a public swimming area with a diving tower and a diving board. The platform of the tower was about twelve feet above the water, and about six feet below the platform was a diving board. At some point during the day, I was up on the platform, and I looked down, and I thought to myself, *You know, if I don't jump onto that diving board, I might just think I'm afraid to do it.* I couldn't stand the thought of that, so I jumped from the platform down to the diving board, and the board bent so far that it almost touched the water. It was a wonder that it didn't snap off, but it just sprung me into the air. It could have thrown me in any direction; fortunately, it threw me out into the pond. Thank goodness! That was the sort of thing I had to prove to myself but once.

Mickey and his siblings during the Depression

Another thing we learned during the Depression was to accept what was doable and not complain about inconveniences. I remember this applying to Elizabeth in one particular incident.

Of all the family, Elizabeth was probably the most outgoing, and she was also very pretty. One time she was in a beauty contest, and my mother was going to make her a gown. It was going to be blue velvet, I think. When Mama cut it out, however, she laid the material so that she had half the cloth cut with the pattern on the wrong side and so the back of the material was entirely different from the front. But Mama was the kind who would say, "I'm putting it together, and it's going to be a different dress, but you can hold your head up."

So my sister wore that dress, and it did not look bad because it had contrasting areas. I'm not sure anybody knew what had happened. My mother didn't say, "I've ruined this dress, so you can't be in the competition." She didn't tell Elizabeth that she could not afford to buy more material. She just told her to hold her head high, and everything would be all right. And Elizabeth never objected. She just assumed that Mama knew what was right.

Father Comes Home

After seven years of long-distance family life, Father, I suppose, got fed up with the situation and finally told the Seed Loan that he was quitting and moving back to South Carolina. Because they didn't want to lose him, they moved him back, and he continued to work for the Seed Loan in South Carolina. That was around 1940 when I was fourteen. It gave us all a deep sense of satisfaction to have him at home all the time.

School Years

I went to public school in Ridge Spring, and I remember a number of wonderful teachers who helped shape my life. Miss Grace Frontis was my teacher in the first grade, Miss Bessie Jones taught me in the second, Mrs. Leila Quattlebaum in the third, Miss Harriet Brunson in the fourth, Mrs. Elizabeth Truluck in the fifth, and my mother in the seventh.

When I graduated from high school, I was in a class of eleven—seven girls and four boys. I also took Latin for two years, which helped me immeasurably with word derivation and in medical school. Even today we use Latin abbreviations when we write prescriptions. Recent medical school graduates write prescriptions in English, but I was taught to use Latin abbreviations. For example, *Signatum* abbreviated *Sig:* means label in Latin. This is followed by the directions for taking the drug. The actual directions are abbreviations of Latin words or phrases.

My mother was an excellent English teacher, and she had always encouraged my interest in reading. Early on, I developed the ability to read very quickly, which came in handy during my medical school years when there was such a huge volume of material to read. Reading came to me as a natural thing. By the time I was in the seventh grade, I had read every book in our school library. I loved to read and to learn. I didn't ask a lot of questions, but I listened. I wanted to understand what other people thought.

I also liked to build up my vocabulary. I remember once, when Elizabeth was at the University of South Carolina, she came home on a holiday and while we were talking, Mama said it was time for supper. So I said to Elizabeth, "Well, I've got to go upstairs and get on with my ablutions."

She looked at me and said, "How did you know that word? We only just studied that."

I could be very affected by my reading or the stories that my mother read to me. If the story was sad (I remember her reading *Black Beauty* in particular), I would say that it made my throat hurt. Well, that, of course, was the lump I would get in my throat from choking back my emotions. I remember Mama telling our minister's wife about that—how my throat would hurt when I heard a sad story. I guess it still does.

Besides my mother, I also had an excellent English teacher in high school—Mrs. Mattie Lee Bonnette. It is hard for me to convey how good she was. When I went to Clemson, many were struggling with English, but I made an A; and without much trouble, because she had already taught me that material. One of the things she did that made a great impression on me and that strikes me even now as being especially insightful was the practical training she gave us in communicating clearly and listening carefully. For instance, she would have every student in the class, one each day, stand up and tell the class how to get to his or her own house. It was great training not only for the person who was giving the directions but also for the people who were listening.

When I first began my medical practice in Bamberg, a young boy called me on the phone to come see his mother, and I said, "I don't know where you live. Tell me how to get to your house." There was a long pause, and finally the boy said, "I can't tell you how to get to my house." And I thought, *you should have been in Mrs. Bonnett's class.*

I think that with my mother's foundation and Mrs. Bonnett's class and the fact that we spoke English correctly in our home, I have never felt uncomfortable using the English language. That has made it easy for me to get up to speak to a crowd, knowing that I didn't have to worry about the English grammar that I use, because I was taught to use correct grammar all the time. I don't remember Mama having to correct any of us very much. Because it was spoken correctly in our home, we used proper English from the very beginning.

My high school had only a basketball team, as we didn't have enough boys to field a football or baseball team. We gave seven-man football a try but failed miserably. Our basketball team was pretty good, though, as we played all year long without regard to football or baseball. As for social activities, belonging to such a small school made us especially close. We did everything together. We had class plays, dancing, elocution, and social "get-togethers."

Father's Wisdom

Although I was a good student and liked learning, I had my rebellious moments like any other adolescent. I remember when

I was in the tenth grade, I decided that I was sick of school and didn't intend to go anymore. Father didn't say a word or even act surprised.

The next morning, though, at five-thirty he came into my room and said, "Get up. If you are not going to school, you have to go to work."

He had ordered two freight cars of loose lime, and they were at the railroad depot. We had two mule-drawn wagons and a truck that we would use to haul the lime to the fields. I drove the truck and took one of our hands along with me, while two other hands drove the two wagons. I got to the depot long before the two wagons, and the hand and I shoveled the lime into the truck. By the time we had loaded the truck, the wagons had arrived, so we helped to load them too. Once all the loading was done, we started back to the field. As before, I arrived first in the truck and the hand and I unloaded. Then the wagons arrived, and we helped unload them. This was repeated over and over throughout that day and the next day as well—hard, dirty, exhausting work. On the third day, I announced that I was returning to the classroom, and the question of quitting high school never came up again.

Mickey's family portrait

Accepting Jesus

Throughout my childhood, religion was an integral part of my family life and the society in which I grew up. My mother was a devout Christian and was very interested in missions. She was active in the local Women's Missionary Society as long as the children were small. As we grew older, she was elected district president of the group. Later, she became president of the Women's Society of Christian Service, a successor organization, which is now The United Methodist Women.

Mama told my wife, Mary Carolyn, that I went to my first Methodist Women's Missionary Society meeting when I was six weeks old. I suppose you could say I cut my teeth on that group. Later in our lives, my brother and I spent a lot of time in missions, and I know Mama smiled down from heaven about that.

I suspect that I was not more than six or seven when Mama saw to it that I was a regular participant in Sunday school. My teacher at that time was an elderly lady by the name of Dr. Anna Barnes. One thing in particular she said has stuck with me for all of these years:

"What you do," she said, "thunders so loud that I can't hear what you say."

For me, this was a more powerful way of saying, "Actions speak louder than words." And I have tried to keep it in mind ever since.

In the summertime, during my years in high school, I attended a Methodist church camp in the mountains. That was a broadening and enriching experience that introduced me to people from all over South Carolina. Coming from such a small farming community, my circle of acquaintances in my own age was very small, so I enjoyed meeting all these new people and participating in all the planned activities. I won several swimming meets and began to learn how to manage my natural shyness.

I have always felt close to God and that He is with me all the time. My mother is responsible for that actually. Even to this day, you know, I pray many times a day, a sentence or two, and I look to Him for guidance. When I was twelve years old, I joined the church and accepted Christ as my Savior. I haven't always pleased Him in my actions, but 95 percent of the time, I believe He would have approved.

Fixing My High School Transcript

During my senior year in high school, (which was eleventh grade at that time), I was accepted at Clemson College, now Clemson University. However, one afternoon during the summer, the school superintendent, Mr. Marbet, called and asked me to come see him. When I arrived, he explained that all of my school records had been lost, and he had to send a transcript to Clemson. So we sat down and I tried to recollect what grades I had made in every class I had taken. Often I couldn't recall them, and in that case he would say, "How did you do in this class?" I would say what I recalled, such as good, very good, etc., and he would assign a letter grade. And so Mr. Marbet and I created the transcript that helped me get into Clemson.

Enlisting as a Marine

World War II and the Marines

I remember well the day that I heard we were at war with Japan. I was in the tenth grade and was hitchhiking back home from Clemson where I had been visiting Joe. A kind man picked me up in Saluda, S.C. He had a car radio, and we listened to the news of the attack on Pearl Harbor as we drove toward Ridge Spring.

Joe at this time was a cadet at Clemson, and I had gone there to watch a football game. Until 1955, Clemson was an all-male military college. I had met Joe and slept in the room of a friend who was away for the weekend. Then I wore the uniform of another friend and walked into the game along with all the other cadets. I'm not sure that Mama knew of all these details, but this was the plan that Joe and I followed. We hadn't exactly told a lie, but we were deceptive.

After the attack on Pearl Harbor, the whole country became extremely patriotic and backed the war effort 100 percent. We accepted the inconveniences, like gasoline rationing with good grace, and we seemed willing to do anything to further the cause. As Mama wasn't teaching anymore (she had stopped when Father returned from Kentucky), I rode the two or three miles to school on a bicycle and delivered several bottles of milk to the grocery store on my way. We had one milk cow and, at that time, only three people were at home—Mama, Father, and me—so we had milk to spare. Mama's frugal nature wouldn't allow her to waste the extra milk, and in those tough times, any small addition to our income was helpful.

For men who were unable to serve in the armed forces, usually older men and boys, the Home Guard was established. I joined, as did many others, but it never seemed to amount to much in Ridge Spring. All we ever did was practice close-order drill. And if there was ever an invasion (and rumors of such would surface from time to time), I really didn't think close-order drill would help.

Enrolling in College, Pondering Enlistment

In the fall of 1943, when I entered Clemson, there were only about 400 civilian cadets enrolled there. The rest of the college was filled with various GI training programs. I was somewhat familiar with the school, as Joe had been there and had told me what to expect. He was attending Officer Candidate School (OCS), however, so I was on my own when I experienced freshman hazing firsthand.

All freshmen were expected to bow down to the upperclassmen and to take whatever hazing was handed out, which sometimes included physical punishment. The big thing during my freshman year was to require the freshmen to bend over and accept a certain number of licks with a broom. I always did what I was told, but from the beginning, I had determined to show no fear. When I was taking licks, I never said anything until it was finished, and then I would say, "Is that the best you can do?" This almost always brought forth another beating, but I was determined that they were not going to intimidate me. This went on for quite a while until one day, when I was in the shower with the company commander (we had communal showers), he took a look at my buttocks, which by that time were deep purple, and issued an order that I was not to be beaten anymore.

I had enrolled in electrical engineering and proceeded with that curriculum. To be honest, though, I didn't give school my best effort at that time. There was so much unrest and uncertainty about the future. It was almost a sure thing that I would be in the armed forces long before I graduated. In fact, the only reason I was not already in the service was that I was seventeen, and my parents had made it quite clear that they were not going to give their permission for me to enlist.

However, as my eighteenth birthday was in January, I knew I would be drafted soon; so I began to think about volunteering, and I did apply for Naval Flight School. I even went to Atlanta for the physical only to be told that my "pigeon-breast" chest deformity disqualified me, as I wouldn't fit a flight harness. Fortunately, I wasn't too disappointed since I didn't particularly care for the idea of air-to-air combat.

As I pondered my future and tried to decide which of the services I should join, two factors influenced my thinking: one was that my mother's only brother (and my only "blood" uncle), Harry Cunningham, had served in the Marine Corps during World War I. Uncle Harry was a wonderful man whom I liked and admired, and so I couldn't help but think that what was good for him would be good for me too. The second factor was a movie called *To The Shores of Tripoli*, starring John Wayne. This movie was a powerful recruiting device, and like a lot of other young men, I pictured myself fighting for America just like the marines in that film. I also toyed with the idea of joining the paratroops and happened to talk with an army paratrooper who was visiting in Ridge Spring. In commenting on how tough the training was, he mentioned that it was nothing compared to the Marine paratroops. Well, that settled it for me. I would volunteer for the Marine Corps and not wait to be drafted.

Joining the Marines

I went to the Marine recruiting office in Columbia and expressed my interest. I was told that I would have to go to the draft board in Saluda (my county seat), and they would send me to Columbia to enlist. Then I would return home for thirty days and report back to the recruiting office. On the designated day, a friend and classmate, Brice Jordan, took me to Saluda. We walked in and were greeted by a clerk who gave me a form to sign, which I did. Then, standing well back from the counter, she said, "You just signed an application for immediate enlistment. You won't be coming back for the thirty days." I never understood why she did that, but in any event, I was on my way.

From Saluda, I was taken to Columbia and sworn in with two other men. Fortunately, the folks at the recruiting office were understanding enough to allow me to go home and say my good-byes. Mama was very apprehensive about her baby going off to face who knew what. Her eyes were moist when I left.

After returning to Columbia, I was put on a Greyhound bus with the other two recruits, and we were shipped off to the recruit depot at Parris Island. Somehow in all my planning, I had never become aware of the term "boot camp" nor of the infamous Parris Island. In the movie, John Wayne had spent a brief period at the recruit depot in San Diego and then gone on to more heroic settings. But during the trip from Columbia, I began to get inklings of what the future might bring. The first thing that made me think that things might not be so rosy was the attitude of the driver as we got closer to the base. All the other passengers had gotten off, and the three of us were the only riders left. He became very solicitous and behaved as if he were carrying us the last mile. Finally, we arrived at our destination. He stopped the bus and politely pointed out a desk under a shed and told us to report to that clerk. That was the last polite thing that happened to us.

Arriving at Parris Island

We got off the bus and went to the clerk who took our names and told us to sit on a bench about ten feet away. There we sat, and having nothing else to do, we took out cigarettes and began to smoke. (In those days, it was generally accepted that most young men smoked.)

Suddenly, we heard a loud voice say, "Who in the g** d*** hell told you people you could smoke!"

I thought to myself, *Somebody is in bad trouble.*

I looked around and saw a short sergeant standing with his feet apart, holding a swagger stick, and looking directly at us! That's when I realized that he was shouting at us.

"Nobody," one of us answered.

The immediate reply was a roaring command.

"Nobody, 'Sir'! And stand at attention when you talk to me!"

By the tone of his voice we knew that we had all better do as he said. Once we were up, another command quickly followed: "Left face. Forward march."

Then he began counting cadence as we marched away, which left us with one slight problem—what to do with the cigarettes. I was convinced it would be death to throw them on the ground, so I put mine out in my hand and shoved it in my pocket.

So much for orientation.

We were marched to a barracks and assigned bunks where we slept that night. At 4:30 AM, a drill instructor came in, roared at us until we got out of bed and ordered us to "fall in" in fifteen minutes outside the barracks. We were then marched to the "delousing" station. (By this time there were about sixty of us.) We were assembled in a large room where we took off all our clothes, wrapped them in brown paper with all our possessions, and addressed them to ourselves at home. They were taken up, and we were herded into several lines and passed by several "barbers" who cut all of our hair to about a quarter of an inch.

From there we went through a large shower and cleaned up. Then we assembled on the other side where various items of clothing were hurled at us. No one asked any size except shoes. We then assembled outside in formation and were marched to our regular barracks. As all of our clothes were missized, we must have been a pathetic sight.

Things only got worse after this. The idea behind boot camp is to thoroughly break men and then remake them into marines who will obey commands instantly, without questions. They did a good job.

The three of us from South Carolina found ourselves with fifty-seven men from Brooklyn, the Bronx, and Connecticut. This was before TV and its leveling effect on regional accents. We could hardly communicate. But we could all understand our drill instructor, the DI, and we knew who he was talking to when he shouted out for "you people." We were almost never called by name, just "you people."

Boot camp was physical in every way and demanded a high level of conditioning. Every day included exercises that were designed to increase our strength, stamina, and willingness to endure hardship. Fortunately, the average age of a marine in World War II was nineteen, and this was reflected in our group with few exceptions. One of the ones who came from Columbia with me was an old man of thirty-two and somewhat overweight. He suffered more than the rest but came through very trim and fit.

A Marine

A Day at Boot Camp

Our day began at 4:30 AM with a wakeup call in the same sort of abusive language in which every message was addressed to the recruits. We were expected to finish in the head (bathroom) in about five minutes and be standing at attention by our bunks. We were constantly berated, and shouts of "Hurry up, expletive," filled the air. The last man to stand at attention was given special attention and his numerous weaknesses were pointed out in the bellowed obscenities of the DIs.

When everyone was in place, the command, "Outside!" was given, along with suitably foul language, describing the speed with which the command was to be executed. Naturally, a big pileup occurred at the door, which was only about four feet wide. Everyone was fighting to get outside while the DIs were yelling at us at the top of their lungs. Outside, there were other DIs again shouting at us to hurry and get in formation and stand at attention. Finally, everyone was in place and we did calisthenics for about thirty minutes. Then we marched to the mess hall. Beware, the man who began the march by stepping off with his right foot. He was singled out for special verbal abuse, as was anyone who did not stay in step or turned right if the command was column left, etc. I thanked my lucky stars for the Home Guard experience and the military training at Clemson.

After eating, we assembled outside and marched to the drill field where we practiced close-order drill for several hours. Perfection was the goal, and each DI was competing with his fellows and wanted to have the best platoon.

The training for the drill was intense, and we had at least an hour of calisthenics each day. We also were given lectures on the history of The Corps and the US Navy, for the marines are considered a branch of the navy. Nautical terms are used throughout the marines, such as *port, starboard, fore,* and *aft* instead of left, right, back, and front. The bathroom was called the *head* and the ground or any other surface that we walked on was the *deck.* The Marine Corps has a proud tradition, and every man was taught to revere this tradition.

Duties

Upon first arriving at Parris Island, each of us was issued a zinc-dipped metal bucket, soap powder, "tie-ties," and a scrub brush. We soon found out what they were used for. Behind each barracks were several concrete tables about six feet wide by eight feet long. Each side sloped toward the center where there was a drain. These were our "washing tables," and here we washed all of our clothes.

On a designated day, we collected around these tables with our dirty clothes and equipment. We soaked the dirty clothes in our buckets, spread them one at a time on the wash table, sprinkled soap powder on them, and scrubbed them with the brush. When they were clean, which meant that our DI had inspected them and declared them clean, we wrung them out and hung them on a clothesline.

This is where our tie-ties came in. When issued, they were a long, stout cotton cord with a pair of metal clips attached about every fourteen inches. We were instructed to cut between each pair of clips to produce several fourteen-inch pieces of cord with a clip at either end so the cord would not unravel. We used these tie-ties instead of clothespins to tie our clothes onto the line.

The bucket was something we carried with us until we were discharged, and we found it useful in a number of ways. For example, we had a sea bag into which we packed all of our clothes. The bucket was put in the sea bag about one-third of the way from the bottom, and it was in the bucket that we stored all our personal items, such as toothbrushes, toothpaste, and shaving equipment.

Along with our clothes, we maintained the quarters in spotless condition, including swabbing the decks daily. It was here where I first learned that white people could clean toilets, which may seem like a peculiar notion now, but I had spent my entire life in a world in which black people did the work that white people considered too lowly to do. It had never crossed my mind that I would be doing such things when I joined the Marines. Although there were no black marines in my day, the Marine Corps had a great social leveling influence on me. No longer was I a product of the upper middle class, I was a nobody in a group of nobodies. This is a lesson I never forgot, and it has helped me tremendously in later life. I remember once treating a man from out of town who became ill while stopping in Bamberg. As it turned out, the man was extremely wealthy, but everyone expected him to receive the same appropriate medical care that the poorest black man would receive. Jack Padgett, Sr., a local pharmacist, said the following to a friend who passed the comment on to me, "I don't care how much money he has. Dr. Watson is going to treat him like everyone else."

In spite of the intensity and rigor of the situation, occasionally something would happen that, looking back, was ridiculous and funny. One morning, we were assembled outside the mess hall, and a recruit hesitatingly held up his hand. The DI shouted, "What do you want?"

"Sir," said the recruit in an apologetic manner, "I've got to go to the bathroom."

The DI swelled up and turned red in the face. Apparently, no one ever had this problem before, and he felt it was totally unnecessary. We recruits waited for the inevitable punishment. Finally the DI roared, "You people will have to learn to control yourselves!" Then he excused the recruit. Such a request never happened again.

The Poncho

An old saying in the Marine Corps: "A marine is never caught without, but a good marine is never caught." As usual, I learned this the hard way.

One morning, just several days after my arrival, we had gone to the mess hall wearing ponchos that we had been issued, as it was raining. When we got inside, we took off our ponchos and ate breakfast. When we had finished, my poncho was gone. I couldn't find it anywhere. I reported this to the DI who said, "Looks like you are going to get wet." And I did. From then on, I got soaking wet every time it rained. One rainy day, as I was leaving the mess hall, I noticed that there were several ponchos that other recruits had left. I picked up one and went outside to fall in with the formation. I noticed that a DI from another platoon was talking to our DI. Our DI turned and shouted, "Watson!"

"Yes, Sir!" I responded.

"Do you have a poncho?"

"Yes, Sir!"

"Bring it here!"

"Yes, Sir!"

And in proper military style, I stepped up and gave my new poncho to the other DI. I tried the same thing on several other occasions with the same results until finally I came across a poncho that no one asked for.

Mike's Marine platoon

Fainting on Parade

I remember on one occasion, there was a fund drive for the Red Cross. The base commander was very anxious to have a hundred percent participation, and he got it. To celebrate, he planned to have all the available recruits assemble on the parade ground in the form of a gigantic cross and the numeral 100%. On the appointed day, we marched onto the parade ground and formed the intended design. Naturally, we were required to stand at attention, and the first platoons in place stood the longest. Now humans cannot stand unflinchingly motionless for very long because their blood will accumulate in their legs, and eventually they will faint. I suspect that is why the position of "Parade Rest" came into being.

After we had been standing at rigid attention for quite a while, I heard a weak voice from the formation say, "Sir, I think I'm going to faint." (The DIs were standing at intervals along the periphery making certain that we were properly lined up.)

The DI nearest the speaker was apparently caught off guard, and he turned to the next DI and said, "This recruit says he's going to faint."

The reply was, "Ah, just wait till the s.o.b. falls." In a few moments, there was a loud clatter of a rifle hitting the asphalt. Within a short time there was another clatter, then another, then several at one time. Recruits were fainting left and right. Before it got any worse, the command "Parade Rest" was passed down the line. I'm sure we made a mess of the commandant's plan.

A Marine and His Rifle

Besides drilling, history lectures, and all our other expected duties, we were taught hand-to-hand combat, knife and club fighting, and the proper use of the bayonet. However, the most important aspect of our training was the care and use of our rifle, which each of us was issued shortly after we arrived. The rifle was almost revered, and it deserved special treatment. Before a recruit ever learned how to fire his rifle, he learned how to take it apart, clean it, and reassemble it. It was to be clean at all times and ready for inspection. We spent hours polishing our rifles so that not even a speck of dust could be found, and we often carried them as we drilled. Sometimes, when the DI considered our drills sloppy, he would order us to fix bayonets to the rifles and then resume the drill. Having a bayonet point turning quickly left and right about six inches from your face increases your awareness immensely.

The recruit who dropped his rifle was to be pitied. After a severe tongue lashing, he was forced to sleep with the rifle in his bunk, which doesn't sound too bad until you realize that the rifle was placed crossways on the mattress. Besides this, the recruit was the subject of special ridicule by the DIs.

After about eight weeks, we were taken to the rifle range where we stayed throughout this portion of boot camp. The rifle range was two or three miles from the recruit depot, and we ran the entire way, of course, in formation. No stops allowed.

At the rifle range, we lived in tents that had wooden floors raised on wooden frames. There were eight men in a tent, and each tent was lighted by a single bare light bulb hanging down from the center. Soon after my squad got to our tents, we discovered that our bulb had burned out. So a couple of us walked to the DI's tent and reported the problem.

"My," he responded sarcastically, "it's going to get dark early for you people, isn't it?"

So in the best marine tradition, we waited until we saw an empty tent with a working light bulb. Then we hurriedly unscrewed it and replaced it with our dead bulb.

Life at the rifle range seemed a little more relaxed than at the recruit depot. The DIs were still around and shouting at us occasionally but not all the time as they had been. Great emphasis was placed on marksmanship, and I suppose they wanted us to focus on that while we were at the range.

Before we ever fired a live round, we were taught the various firing positions—standing, sitting, kneeling, and prone. Each recruit had a coach to watch and criticize the various positions that we assumed. After learning the positions, we began "snap in" drills. These drills took the recruit through all the steps required to assume a position and then fire but with no cartridges in the rifle. When we pulled the trigger, the rifle just snapped. When learning to fire, great emphasis was placed on squeezing rather than jerking the trigger. Jerking the trigger, we learned, would almost invariably cause the shooter to miss the target.

After several boring days of these snap in drills, we finally went to the firing range. Here we were given live ammunition for the first time and were allowed to fire. The targets were at various distances, and we became comfortable shooting at all of them from all the different positions. One of the things that I remember very vividly was watching the trajectory of a bullet as it went over one of the longer distances and hit the target. It's hard to imagine being able to watch something as fast and small as a bullet flying through the air, but it could be done, though only by the man who fired the bullet or by someone crouched immediately behind him.

Except for the pressure of becoming "qualified" with the rifle, which meant passing the corps' competency rating, the rifle range was generally a pleasant relief from the harsh life at the depot. We were understandably disappointed when the day came that we had finished our rifle training and had to return to the depot, which we did, of course, at a run and in formation.

Guard Duty

Almost everything we learned in boot camp, we learned by doing, and another of those things that we learned was guard duty. This is a very important function of the Marine Corps. A cadre of US Marines guards virtually all US naval stations and US foreign service stations, such as embassies, whether on US or on foreign soil. The reason for this role is that The Corps is part of the navy and as such is permitted to operate on foreign soil without a declaration of war, which is not something the army is allowed to do. During the war, sailors held the marines in low regard, as the marines were far more strict than the navy. Many a sailor being checked out to go on liberty was sent back to his station by a marine guard at the gate who would not let the sailor off base until the sailor had put his uniform in order.

On Parris Island, we performed guard duty as if the enemy were lying just off shore and would be landing at any moment. I remember on one occasion, a member of my detail committed a minor infraction (if there is any such thing in the Marine Corps); and for punishment, the entire detail was made to walk guard, go on duty all night in the salt marsh that surrounds the facility. This was easily the longest night I have ever spent. As I walked back and forth, ankle-deep in marsh mud, I had plenty of time to reflect on the injustice of my being punished for something that I had not done. But that was part of marine training—to teach us that in combat, an error made by one man, even a slight error, can bring disaster down on everyone else in that man's unit.

A Troubling Encounter

Toward the end of my tour at Parris Island, one of the company clerks asked me to go to a movie with him. This was very unusual, as we ordinarily did not have an opportunity to go to movies, the post exchange, or anywhere else. I did not know him, but the chance to get away from the barracks sounded good to me. So we walked to the movie, and afterward, as we were walking back, we passed by an empty barracks, and he suggested that we go inside and talk. So we went inside and lay down on some mattresses that were piled up at one end of the room. Before long, he began to get closer to me until finally he was lying with his head on my leg, and he began to stroke me. At this point, I had no idea what was happening, but I decided I had better get myself out of that situation and go back to the barracks.

The next day, having mulled all I could over the situation, I went to my friend, Eddie Wollert, who was a product of the streets of Bridgeport, Connecticut, and, by my standards, a man of vast worldly experience. When I told Eddie about the strange behavior I had encountered the day before, his reaction was to laugh until he cried. He couldn't believe that anyone could live to be eighteen years old and still be so innocent. Finally, though, after recovering from his mirth, he explained homosexuality to me in the graphic language of adolescence. And he told me what the situation had meant, which left me shocked and disgusted but far more worldly-wise, or so I thought.

Sometime after the war, my brother Joe and I met in Columbia (I've forgotten what the occasion was), and we went to a restaurant for dinner. As Joe and I were sitting together, this obviously gay man came over and started to come on to me. By this time, though, I was an experienced marine and not to be trifled with. So I said, "Buddy, how about leaving us alone."

But he kept on.

So I said, "If you don't leave us alone, I'm going to bust you in the mouth."

That got rid of him. Joe, however, was stunned.

"Why did you act that way? He was just being polite."

"Joe, that man was a queer."

Joe was as innocent as I had been. He had no idea what had been going on.

Many years later, when dealing with homosexual AIDS patients, I learned to look at gay people in an entirely different way. I had to step beyond the superficial way I had looked at things when I was younger. Today I always try to give gay AIDS patients a sympathetic touch and to hug them whenever it's appropriate. As this became a regular habit of mine, I remember thinking once, *What in the world could bring a man, who thought about homosexuals as I once did, to hug someone who is gay? Only the Holy Spirit. Only the Holy Spirit.*

As a Marine

Mike in Marine service uniform

Advanced Training and the Pacific

In the final days at Parris Island, we were given an extensive battery of psychological and aptitude tests. After we had finished, we had a session with a counselor to complete the evaluation process. At this point in my processing, the counselor asked what specialty I wanted. I explained that I had enlisted to join the paratroopers.

"No," he said, "your IQ is much too high for that. I'm putting you down for electronics school."

This was the last thing that I wanted to hear. I tried to explain to him that I had just come out of school and had no intention of going back in. He could not be dissuaded, however, but finally said, "Now I'm going to have to put this down, but if you flunk out, then they will have to send you somewhere else."

I resolved right then that flunking out was exactly what I would do.

Moonshine

There was no graduation ceremony or anything else when we finished boot camp. We just got up one morning and were taken to Yemassee, a small town just over the waterway from Parris Island. There we boarded a train for Camp Lejeune, North Carolina where we would receive our advanced instruction.

When we got on the train, another young marine said to me, "Man, did I get a deal." He was grinning all over himself.

"What's that?"

He held up a glass jar for us to see and said, "I got here the best bootleg moonshine that you have ever tasted. A fella just sold it to me at the depot. Look at that. Clear as water."

"How do you know it's moonshine?"

"I tasted it," he answered.

Then to show me, he unscrewed the top and raised it to his lips. With an expletive, he spewed it out. The bottles had been switched on him. All he had in his jar was pure water, which was better for him anyway, although I'm sure he didn't think so at the time.

Camp Lejeune

I found Camp Lejeune a welcome relief from Parris Island. To be sure, there was still discipline like iron but no intimidation. People were actually civil to each other. I was put in a barracks with sixty others and each wall was lined with double-decker bunks. As I was settling in, I saw an "old-timer" who was already in electronics school. I approached him and asked, "How long does it take to flunk out of this place?"

"You can't flunk out," he told me. "They know that you have the IQ to pass. The course is divided into monthly segments. If you flunk one month, you will just repeat it until you pass. The quickest way to get out of here is to study hard and pass each time."

This was not what I had wanted to hear, but I resigned myself to studying as hard as I could so that I could get out and perhaps transfer into something else. I didn't know what I wanted to do, as I had heard that the paratroops had been disbanded. It seems that in the invasion of Guadalcanal, paratroopers were deployed as part of the assault team, and most of them landed in trees where the Japanese easily killed them.

The next morning, I was in class at eight o'clock with about twenty other students. We all studied and attended class together in one group. This was in the dawn of the electronics boom, and we were at the forefront of what was known about electronics at that time. It was not like any other school I had ever attended. The classes were from 8 AM until 8 PM. There were no textbooks. In essence, we wrote our own textbooks from the notes we took in class. The material in our notebooks was classified as "secret," and our schoolroom was in a restricted area that was under twenty-four-hour armed guard. Each morning, we checked our notebooks out of the confidential library and went to class for the day. At the conclusion of each day, we checked our notebooks back into the confidential library before we left the compound.

When I was transferred to my next assignment, I traveled by troopship, but my notebooks were checked out of the library by an armed courier who traveled by air and checked my notebooks into the confidential library on the base that was my destination. Only when I was finally assigned to a unit overseas was I allowed to keep them with me.

The objective of this school was to qualify us for the military occupational specialty (MOS) number of 775. This number meant that we would be qualified to maintain and operate any electronic equipment owned by the Marine Corps. Our emphasis, however, was on radar (Radio Detection And Ranging), which was very new at that time and the reason for all the heavy security measures.

Scuttlebutt had it that we would study the same amount of electronics information as was in a PhD program. We had no "frills" such as advanced physics and mathematics except in instances when it was necessary for understanding, which was seldom. In essence, we covered all the raw applied electronics known at that time, including information about all electronic equipment then in use. The information was voluminous, and the training was intense. One skill I developed that was valuable then and has been for the rest of my life was learning to take notes in narrative form. After a while, the information presented simply flowed through my head and onto the paper in a condensed and accurate form. I don't believe that I could have done as well as I did in medical school without this background.

Electronics school became my life. It consumed me. I lived and breathed electronic theory and thought of little else. When I went back to the barracks in the evening, I had no newspapers or radio to distract me. There was little communication between students, as we were forbidden to talk about what we had learned. Often I would go to bed while still mulling over a part of electronics theory that I didn't understand and then wake up in the middle of the night when the solution would come to me. Then I would go right back to sleep. On the rare occasions that I had a weekend leave to go home, all I thought about on the long bus ride to Ridge Spring was electronic theory. When I got home, it was difficult to talk to anybody, as all I had been thinking about was electronics, and no one would understand that. Sometimes a thought would hit me while I was with a group of friends, and I would have a tremendous urge to talk about it, but then I would assume that the others would think I had lost my mind.

This school lasted about ten months and included a four-week course in gasoline and diesel engines, as some of the equipment could be carried on bicycle carts and had small portable power plants. We had to learn how to maintain and operate that equipment as well.

We had one new long-range unit that had an output of one million watts, which was unprecedented in those days. At night, we could aim the antenna at an office building, and all the fluorescent lights in the entire building would light up. There was so much scatter radiation around the unit that you could simply hold a fluorescent tube in your hand and it would be illuminated from scatter radiation as you walked within a thirty-foot radius. When I was in medical school some years later and we were studying the effects of radiation, I told a professor about this experience. His response was disconcerting.

"I'm sorry," he said, "but you have probably received a mutating dose of radiation."

This was not good news, and it had implications not only for me, but for any children that might come along. Later I learned, to my relief, these implications applied only to *ionizing* radiation and not to radio energy.

Of the thirty to forty students who began the session, only nine completed it successfully, which refutes the old-timer's assertion that no one flunked out. The ones who washed out went into subspecialty schools, usually to become radio operators or radio technicians and were not given specialty 775 numbers.

I stuck it out for several reasons. One was that I hate to fail at anything. Another, probably even more important, was that I became intensely interested in the subject. I had always been curious about electronics, which was the main reason I went into electrical engineering at Clemson, and the electronics school gave me the opportunity to explore the topic thoroughly.

At Camp Lejeune, North Carolina

Awaiting Transfer Overseas

After I finished school, I was made PFC and sent to "Tent City" to await transfer overseas. At Hadnot Point, where the Signal Battalion was located, I had been in a nice new steam-heated barracks made of brick. Tent City, on the other hand, was exactly what the name implies—a large group of tents, unheated, with crude central bathing and toilet facilities. I believe the leadership used wartime economics to prepare for peacetime operations. They didn't erect any prefabs that would have to be torn down at the end of the war, just some tents.

Sleeping in a tent without heat in January is bracing, to say the least. In fact, it was downright cold! We went day after day without ever getting warm. There were eight of us per tent, and we tried everything we could think of to get warm. We had two wool blankets each, which were not nearly enough, particularly since the bottom of the canvas cots provided no barrier to the penetrating cold. Adding sheets of newspaper to the blankets helped some. Finally, one of the men put some sand in his bucket, poured in some fuel oil, and lighted it. Black, oily smoke billowed out of the bucket, but it provided some heat. Soon, however, festoons of soot hung down from the ceiling of the tent, and the slightest movement would bring innumerable black particles showering down.

This misery lasted about two weeks before we were at last transported to Norfolk, Virginia to board a troop transport. A few days prior to leaving, we were turned out in full uniform for review. We stood in formation on the parade ground for what seemed hours but probably was not that long. Soon the review team appeared, leading a Cadillac convertible with an elderly man in the back and a small dog. The commander introduced the president of the United States, and we stood rigidly at attention. The little dog got out and wet on the rear wheel and got back in.

The commander announced, "The President says, 'Best wishes and get a Jap for me!'"

An irreverent voice from the rear ranks replied, "Come with us and get one for yourself!"

I expected lightning to strike him, but it didn't; and no one knew where the reply came from, so there was no punishment.

Shipping Out

Norfolk was cold and rainy. We were herded onto a ship and assigned bunks. The ship, named the USS Florence Nightingale, as I remember, was a banana boat converted to a troop transport by suspending bunks in the holds. My bunk was about fifth from the bottom in a seven-high stack suspended from the overhead with chains. The distance between bunks was about eighteen inches. This meant that you had a choice of sleeping on your stomach or back, as your shoulders were too wide to fit sideways between your bunk and the one above you. Once you were on your stomach or back, if you wanted to change, you had to get out and back in the other way. I quickly learned to get in on my back and stayed that way until the next morning.

After weighing anchor, we pulled out into the North Atlantic, which was cold and rough. Our first meal on board included blueberry pie. As the ship pitched and tossed, almost a hundred percent of the troops became seasick. The rumor circulated that the blueberry pie was planned so that on their cleanup rounds, the crew could easily spot where people had vomited. As for myself, I can testify that there is nothing worse than being young, seasick, and homesick all at the same time! I was one miserable mortal.

We could tell by the sun that we were sailing south, but our destination was unknown. Everyone assumed we were going to the Pacific as that's where the marines were fighting. A few days into our journey, we turned west. The air became hot and humid, and water dripped continuously from the overhead. In addition to having woefully inadequate facilities for brushing teeth or washing clothes, fresh water was at a premium, so the only showers available were saltwater showers. We were issued saltwater soap, but it was worthless.

On day five, we began to see land and then palm trees. We had reached Panama and soon entered the Panama Canal. It was so nice to be rid of those rolling swales and not to feel seasick for a while. It was odd too after all those days on this seafaring ship, seeing nothing but ocean and sky, to find ourselves steaming past people's houses. We looked wistfully at the shore, which seemed very beautiful in its lush tropical greenery and its clean white buildings. For some of us, unfortunately, that only added to our homesickness.

Part of the canal runs through Gatun Lake, which is a freshwater lake. So while we were there amidst all that fresh water, the navy rigged up a raised pipe into which they drilled holes and ran across the deck. Then they pumped fresh water through it, and we would go up there, take off all our clothes, and have a shower. It was great. Some people took two or three showers a day, but not Eddie Wollert, who had shipped out with me. Eddie had wiry hair that no comb would run through, and he liked the saltwater showers because for the first time in his life, he told me he was able to comb his hair and it looked like it; the salt kept it in place.

Soon we went through two more locks and passed into the Pacific Ocean. This was better than the rough Atlantic and generally was smooth, which was a relief. We were to be on this leg of the trip for fourteen days, making a twenty-one day voyage, which introduced us to a common experience of the war—boredom. A small group of us began to get together and meet at a certain spot on the deck and play cards. I believe the game was Queens. Every day we played from morning until night, day after day. One day, one of the men just couldn't stand it anymore. He leaped up and threw the cards over the side of the ship and into the sea. We were stunned, as this was the only deck of cards we had, but we understood—enough is enough.

Things were so boring that I disobeyed one of the pieces of advice my brother, Joe, gave me when I was going into the service: "Keep your mouth shut and volunteer for nothing." One day, one of the cooks came out on deck and said, "I need a volunteer."

"Here," I shouted and jumped up to go with him.

He led me down into the bakery and said that he wanted several large baskets of fresh bread carried to another part of the ship. He counted them as he filled the large basket, and I went to do as he said, my mind going at top speed. The entire time I was on that ship I was hungry—except when I was feeling seasick. In fact, over the course of the entire voyage, I lost twenty-five pounds. The mess hall was much too small for the number of troops on board, and we were given only two meals a day. Everything was boiled—except for the fresh baked bread. As I carried my baskets of bread, I found Eddie Wollert and hurriedly told him to meet me at a certain place. Then I delivered the bread and went back for the next load. This time, I helped place the bread in the large baskets so the baker's count became totally inaccurate, and he eventually gave up and stopped counting. Then I headed off for my next delivery. When I passed by Eddie, I gave him two loaves of bread. The next trip, I managed to stand by a basket of bread that had been trimmed from loaves for the officer's mess. When no one was looking, I filled both of my jacket pockets.

When I had finished my detail, I found Eddie and got one of the loaves. We were careful that no one saw us, as some would have tried to take it away from us. I wormed my way under one of the landing craft on the deck, and there, where no one could see me, I wolfed down the loaf and the two pockets full of bread. Man, what a grand feeling to be full again! Afterward, I got a drink of water, which apparently caused the bread to swell, and then I became achingly full! But in my mind, it was better too full than not full enough.

In Oahu, Hawaii as a Marine with sister
Elizabeth, a Red Cross volunteer

Oahu

Finally, we made port and were taken to the rest and reassignment base. There we were given our mail that had accumulated
while we were at sea. No one had any idea as to where we were,
as we hadn't been told where we were going or where we were
when we got there. As I was sitting on the ground reading my
mail, I discovered from one of my letters that my sister Elizabeth,
who was in the Red Cross, had been stationed in a place called
Oahu. I told this to whoever was sitting next to me, and just then
I looked up and saw a train go by with the words "Oahu Special"

on the side. This was how I found out we had landed on the Hawaiian island of Oahu.

I went to the chaplain's office, and a lady there located Elizabeth and handed me the telephone. We talked for a long time. She was astonished to hear my voice. I got her telephone number and promised to call her when I could get off the base and meet her for lunch.

When I was finally able to get a pass, I called and made a date to meet her. On the way, I stopped in a five- and ten-cent store and bought a transparency that children love to stick on themselves. I picked out one that looked like a tattoo and stuck it on my forearm. Soon after we met she spotted the "tattoo" and looked like she might faint. I hurriedly took it off, and she was much relieved.

We walked around Honolulu and then had lunch. During lunch, I learned that she was working as a secretary in one of the Red Cross offices and entertaining the troops by being a hostess at some of the dances. During the conversation she said, "I have met several All-American football players, but you know," she added in a somewhat disparaging tone, "They're typical All-American football players." One of these football players was John Tandy whom she later married.

The R&R center was not a beehive of activity for marines who were there temporarily, awaiting reassignment. There were thousands and thousands of men with nothing to do. The main activity was going to the PX for a snack ("porgy bait" to Marines—a term for non-nutritious food, i.e., fish bait, thought by the "Old Corps" to impair your vision and reduce your accuracy with the rifle). As the PX was the only source of recreation on the base, it was always crowded and there was always a long line. Everything that was offered was in a single line, which meant that if you wanted something to eat, you had to get everything in one trip or stand in line all over again. Two items that were often bought in this line were steaming hot coffee and ice cream. This was not a good thing, as it forced you to eat the ice cream and drink the coffee together; otherwise, the coffee would get cold or the ice cream would melt. Almost everyone felt that eating the two together was bad for your teeth, but getting them separately meant waiting in the line twice.

One Marine scoffed at the idea of the conflict between the hot and cold foods, and he would take a bite of ice cream and follow it with a drink of hot coffee. Shortly before we were due to depart, we were sitting at the PX talking and eating when suddenly, he reached in his mouth and brought out fragments of both front teeth. They had simply broken off. I don't know the condition of his teeth before this, but the incident certainly was a graphic lesson. When the rest of us shipped out, he had to remain behind to have his teeth fixed.

When we finally got the news that we were shipping out, our destination was unknown. On the appointed day, we found ourselves on another troopship with Spartan living conditions but far better than those on the *USS Florence Nightingale*. We left from Pearl Harbor and passed the wreckage of the battleship *USS Arizona*, a casualty of the Japanese attack on December 7, 1941.

The long voyage of twenty days was briefly interrupted by a stop at the island of Eniwetok. There we were disembarked for several hours just to stretch our legs and walk around. Then we were put back on the ship and resumed the trip. I have no idea what the reasoning was behind the stop; I can't imagine they were thinking of our comfort. There surely was another reason, but the island was little more than a large mound of sand and palm trees in the middle of the ocean, so it was hard to fathom any purpose for stopping there. I read later that one of the earlier nuclear bomb tests was conducted at Eniwetok, and it almost obliterated the island.

Guam

When we arrived at our final destination, we climbed down cargo nets into waiting assault crafts and were taken ashore. There we learned we were on the island of Guam and that we were several months behind the initial assault troops that had secured the island from the Japanese. I was assigned to a searchlight battery and taken to my unit, high on top of a small mountain. The weather there was mild, not blistering hot as were other places on the island, as Guam is ten degrees above the equator.

After several months, I was transferred to a unit of about fifteen men stationed on the beach. There it was steamy hot, day and night, and boredom soon set in. We could not swim in the ocean because to get to an area deep enough to swim, we had to walk about half mile in knee-deep water, stepping all the while on raw coral that would slice bare feet. One time, I wore my shoes and walked out the half mile to the place where the coral shelf fell off. The drop was immediate and precipitous. I had no idea how deep the water was, which gave me a peculiar feeling—to be swimming in this huge expanse of water and not know what was beneath me. I didn't do that again.

We played volleyball endlessly, and for diversion, we began to raise the net until finally the bottom of the net was about eight feet from the ground.

We did only limited walking around as there were many Japanese soldiers still unaccounted for on the island. It was the strategy of the marines to land on an island and fight their way across to the other side, cutting the Japanese forces into two segments and then start dealing with each disorganized segment. This strategy left pockets of armed but isolated enemy soldiers all over the island. Helicopters flew overhead looking for them, and when they were spotted, patrols were dispatched to neutralize them. Little effort was made to capture any of them, as they refused to surrender, so they were largely shot on sight. Some years after the war ended, I read a book, *The Emperor's Last Soldier*, by a Japanese soldier who hid in a cave on Guam for seven years after the war ended, for he had no way of knowing the war was over.

We did walk about a little bit, though cautiously and never alone. The native people were Chamorros, who were small brown people and few in number. There was little if any exchange between the native people and the occupying forces. We had no instructions as to how to proceed, so we didn't. I did see something that I had seen earlier in a *Ripley's Believe It or Not* column. That was a small fish that had large pectoral fins that it would use to pull itself out of the water and walk around on land, usually to get from one water hole to the next.

It was on Guam that many bombers were stationed to carry out the aerial assault on Japan, so the air traffic was heavy on the island. Each plane was equipped with a piece of radio equipment called the IFF, which stood for Identification: Friend or Foe. When a radar beam hit the plane, it triggered this device to send back a signal, which appeared on the radar screen as a small blip and identified the plane as friendly. This device was manually turned off when leaving friendly areas and turned back on when approaching a friendly base. Occasionally, the crew would forget to turn it back on. To those of us on the ground watching the approach on radar, this blip without an IFF signal was an enemy plane. Each time this happened, at the last minute before the antiaircraft firing began, an order was given to the searchlight battery: "Illuminate." The searchlights, which had been tracking the plane the entire time, were turned on and the plane would be pinned by the intense glare of several searchlights. The IFF immediately came on, and we relaxed, knowing that this was not a Japanese bomber. I imagine the crew of the bomber passed a scary moment as well.

In February and March of 1945, sea traffic picked up remarkably as hospital ships came in and transferred their wounded to land-based hospitals on Guam. These ships carried an unbelievable number of wounded men, and it took hours for them to disembark their passengers. We learned that the fighting was on Iwo Jima, a small island to the north of us and about halfway to Japan. For the marines, Iwo Jima was the single bloodiest battle of the war so far.

VE Day and Reassignment

May 7, 1945 was VE Day (Victory in Europe), and when Germany's surrender was announced to us, I remember how relieved I was as I felt then that my brother, Joe, was safe. I didn't know he had been wounded several months earlier in The Battle of the Bulge.

Not long after VE Day, we began to hear scuttlebutt that we were being reassigned to an assault company to participate in the long anticipated invasion of Japan. We heard that we would participate in the third wave of the invasion. We knew that this was a risky position in an invasion, as the Japanese were known to withhold their fire for the first two waves to avoid giving away their gun positions too early. But when the third wave was launched, the firing began, and the third wave was the most vulnerable as it was completely exposed. Besides the scuttlebutt, some new equipment added credibility to the tales we were hearing. We were issued oiled-silk rifle covers, which were designed to protect rifles from saltwater as the assault waves went into shore. You could fire the rifle through the cover on the way in and then take it off later to reload.

This reassignment did not come as a complete surprise, as all marines are trained as line personnel and then given specialty training. Then, without warning, orders came down for me and me alone in the unit to be reassigned. I was taken to the docks and put on board a small aircraft carrier and soon departed Guam. Naturally scuttlebutt was flying, but it soon seemed that the situation was this. In the intense fighting on Iwo Jima, the Marine

Corps had lost over 2,000 second lieutenants. Traditionally, they served as platoon leaders and were in the most exposed position. To replace them, requirements for OCS were lowered to an eighth-grade education and 20/20 vision. This move still did not attract enough candidates, so the decision was made to assign some of those men with high IQs to OCS. This was a historic decision, as officer candidates had always been volunteers before.

Living conditions on the aircraft carrier were several steps above any that I had before and light-years above those I had endured aboard the *USS Florence Nightingale*. As we drew close to the US, the PA system began to carry radio programs from commercial radio stations. I remember how strange singing commercials sounded. The first one I heard was for Pepsi Cola.

The War Is Over

After about a week at sea, the announcement was made that an atomic bomb had been dropped on Hiroshima, causing widespread destruction. Considering the alternative of our having to invade Japan, with casualties expected to be as high as one million, the news of the bomb was welcome indeed, and speculation ran wild as to the implications for all of us servicemen. After eighteen days at sea, we landed at San Diego and were put in temporary quarters at the marine station. A few days later, we got the welcome news of the surrender of Japan.

After that, all the talk was about going home although no one knew when we might go. The radio began reporting demonstrations at a number of army posts by troops who were anxious to be discharged. I heard that a small crowd of discontented marines gathered at one marine post and a general came to speak to them. He stood up and said, "There will be no demonstrations at any marine post." Then he stepped down. There were no demonstrations.

After what seemed to be a long delay, I was put on a troop train and started east. Conditions were tolerable but anything would have been, as we were *going home*! After a few days, things improved greatly when I was moved to a regular, commercial train. I couldn't get over being waited on in the dining car! I believe the entire trip took six or seven days.

I arrived in the train station in Columbia and called home to say I had a thirty-day leave. This was the first time they had heard from me, and when Mama answered the phone, she was over-joyed. They sent Bennie Raiford to get me, and he was a sight for sore eyes. His joy at seeing me was obvious, and my joy at seeing him was the same. Within a couple of hours, I was home and greeting Mama and Father.

The thirty days went by far too fast, but on the other hand, things had changed (or perhaps I had changed), and in many ways, I felt like an outsider. The biggest change for me was in my peers. The girls I had left behind were now young ladies while I, socially at least, still felt like a boy. There is still that gap there of what the late teens and early twenties should have been. It's lost forever.

My boyhood sweetheart, Patty Steadman, was now going steady with a seminary student, which cast me adrift. She and some of my other girl friends tried to fix me up with someone, but nothing came of this effort, as I was so ill at ease and restless.

Soon I was back at Camp Lejeune and the Signal Battalion. I was assigned to work in a radio repair shop and got back into electronics, which was very easy. After a time, I was reassigned to teach in a radio school. I lectured for one hour and was free the rest of the day, and so my old friend boredom returned. The classrooms were located several miles from the barracks, so each day, I sat and talked with the other instructors and drank gallons of coffee.

Promotion to Corporal and Discharge

The high point of my stay was being promoted to corporal. This was a significant step, as I had been the senior Pfc. in the battalion. In the Marine Corps, seniority means everything. It means that you can give orders not only to those with grade levels below yours but even to whoever is at the same grade level but received their warrant after you. As senior Pfc., it was difficult for anyone to give me orders that I couldn't pass on to someone else, so they usually didn't give them to me.

The process in receiving the warrant to corporal was demanding. First, I had to be recommended, and then take a test in my specialty area and in the line duties of a corporal. Then I had to have several interviews.

After receiving my warrant, I found out that there was a number assigned to each person being promoted that day and that the person named with a higher number was senior to all others. My number was "1," meaning I was senior to all other corporals who were promoted that day in the Marine Corps.

Finally, I was issued my discharge and was processed out of the marines. As I was leaving the base, just prior to boarding the bus, I passed by a desk where a sergeant was seated. Behind him was a sign reading "Marine Corps Reserve." When he saw me, he said, "Come on over here, marine, and join the Reserve."

This was the last thing I wanted to do, so I looked at him and said, "Aw, shut up."

This did not get a pleasant response.

"You watch your mouth, marine," said the sergeant. "You are still in the Corps for twenty-four hours after that discharge is signed!"

This was a scary thought, but even so, he couldn't dampen my spirits. My career in the US Marine Corps was over!

At Clemson again—as a veteran student

UNDERGRADUATE YEARS

Pondering a Career

After I was discharged from the Marine Corps, I assumed that I would return to college, but I wasn't certain what I wanted to study. People kept telling me how fortunate I was that I had received so much intensive training in something as useful as electronics, so enrolling in the electrical engineering program at Clemson seemed like the practical thing to do.

Returning to Clemson as a veteran was quite different from my earlier experience as a seventeen-year-old cadet. We veteran students were not in the cadet corps at all. We simply went to class and could use our own discretion regarding study time or anything else. In general, we were a much more serious group than the students who were right out of high school. I would be remiss not to mention the extraordinary benefits provided by the GI Bill of Rights.

Through undergraduate school and three years of medical school, my educational expenses were fully paid, and I was given a small living allowance, which permitted me a certain level of financial independence. I didn't live like a king, but I got by, and I am truly grateful. It was not until my last year in medical school that I had to turn to my father for help with expenses.

After completing my first year back at Clemson, however, I was told that the electronics courses I had taken in the Marine Corps covered everything offered at Clemson in the bachelor degree programs. To learn anything new, I would have to go into a doctoral program, but before I could be accepted in a doctoral program, I would have to complete all the electronics courses in the bachelors program; that is, I would have to repeat everything I had already learned.

This gave rise to some hard thinking about my future. Growing up on a farm, I had learned my share about mechanics and other gadgetry, and I had always taken pleasure in fixing things. Basic electricity was fairly simple, and I had learned that by the time I joined the marines. My marine training then filled in the gaps in my knowledge about such things as vacuum tubes and radio communication. I was grateful for the training, but it had fully satisfied my curiosity about radio and electronics. I didn't want to spend the rest of my life doing what electrical engineers do, and I was not carried away with the idea of entering a doctoral program and adding three more years of school after college.

So there I was in a quandary as to the direction of my future. During the school year, I had gone home often to visit and was interested in Joe's lifestyle. He had married his childhood sweetheart and was living in a small house that the family owned and that he and I had painted and refurbished. He was farming the family land, which I'm sure Father found helpful, and was doing quite well. Besides, I knew that he loved his work.

Therefore, when I arrived home for the summer, I announced that I was changing my major to agriculture and would be staying in Ridge Spring during the summer to learn more about farming. Father didn't object to this or offer any advice. I'm sure that he realized that I had never shown much interest in farming. Up to that point in my life, watching things grow interested me about as much as having a root canal. I had openly disliked farm work and found it extremely boring. But being uncertain what else to do with my life, I suppose I was willing to ignore my past experience and give farming another chance.

Joe the Farmer

As opposed to my dilemma, Joe was fortunate. He had always known that farming was the thing for him. From the time he was a young teenager, Joe was working in the fields right alongside the black men. In fact, he had a special relationship with the hands. He would go to the tenant houses in our backyard, and he would play pool, which was a game on a checkerboard. He would play with them in their homes and get all involved in it. I remember one time, they had opened some scuppernong wine, and when he came home he was tipsy. Before he went to bed, Father saw him, and Father was mighty upset. Father had seen his own younger brother die of alcoholism, so he didn't have much patience with imbibing of any sort. The next morning, while Joe must have been hung over and already feeling mighty bad, Father said, "Joe, let me tell you something. When you get in that condition again, don't you ever come back home." And he meant it.

Given my lack of interest in farming before this time, I was grateful that Joe was willing to let me help him as I gave it a try. I remember at one point, Father bought a combine, one that was pulled by a tractor, and Joe and I decided that we could help Father pay for it by cutting other people's wheat. Well, Joe just loved doing that work. However, I was back there sitting on that combine with all that dust blowing up in my face and eyes and hair, and he just couldn't understand why I wasn't thrilled to death to be doing that. He made it no secret that he thought I was lazy. I suppose that was the only reason he could imagine for someone not wanting to be a farmer.

After the war and after he had finished Clemson, Joe bought a tractor of his own. Joe and that tractor and no one else farmed his land, perhaps a hundred acres. He did everything himself because that tractor could do everything he needed done. And my father, who was a gentleman farmer, was just amazed that Joe would do such a thing. I can't say he was completely surprised, because Joe had always been inclined to do such work.

Father: The Gentleman Farmer

To give an example of the difference between Joe's and Father's attitudes, I remember one time, I was driving one of my father's trucks through Ridge Spring, and I saw him standing in front of the garage where he was having his car worked on, so I asked him if he needed a ride home.

He said, "Well yes, I do."

He got in, and we went down the road. As we were driving along, something struck me, and I said, "You've never been in this truck, have you?" This was a truck that we had owned for four or five years. He shook his head and said, no, he never had. A gentleman farmer simply didn't go around riding in trucks. That was my father's attitude.

Farming, however, was changing, and Joe was right on top of all the latest developments.

Choosing a Career

Not long after I had returned home for the summer and announced my intention to learn farming, Father put me to work. The first chore he had for me was to do some harrowing, so early the next morning as the sun was just coming up, I found myself on a tractor in a peach orchard. At dinnertime (in the rural South it is called dinner, not lunch), Father sent one of the hands out to relieve me while I went to eat. After thirty minutes, I was back on the tractor until it got too dark to see.

This, along with the work that I was doing with Joe, gave me the opportunity to do some more hard thinking, and before many days had passed, I became convinced that I had arrived at my plan to make a career in agriculture too quickly. What then? I now knew two careers that I did *not* want to pursue but not one that seemed very attractive.

That's when Father made a suggestion. A few years before, he had surgery for cancer of the nose that had become fairly far advanced. The surgery was done in St. Louis by a pioneer in plastic surgery. Mama was not able, financially, to be with him during the surgery and hospitalization. He told her, when he returned, that as he was recovering from the anesthesia, a nurse was holding his hand. Later, the nurse told him that he kept calling her Aurelia. Father rightly felt that the surgeon had saved his life, and he was very grateful to him. So about the middle of the summer, he said to me, "I always hoped that you would study medicine and be a doctor." He had never mentioned this before.

I began to think about this. I had thought about doing this many times but had always rejected the idea. The reason was that one of the older boys in Ridge Spring, who I felt was much smarter than I, had started out at Clemson in premed and had flunked organic chemistry several times. It was considered one of the hardest courses in the school but a necessary requirement for admission to medical school. Thinking that if he couldn't pass organic chemistry, then there was no way that I could, I had discarded the thought of medicine as a career almost immediately.

However, being on that tractor all day during that long hot summer gave me plenty of thinking time, so I began to give the idea of medical school serious thought. I knew that a physician's life was hard, but I had never turned away from any task simply because it was hard, so that was no problem. Further, I felt that a physician's life would probably be gratifying, and the opportunity to help people was probably the fundamental attraction. Besides that, I had always been a curious person, and the thought of learning how humans tick on a basic level was intriguing. The fact that most physicians are held in high esteem and frequently take on a valued social station in their communities was another possible benefit. And then there were the possibilities for financial rewards, which actually came in last.

I had a lot of time to think over all the possibilities, and before long, the thought of a career in medicine grew more attractive to me. But I still wondered whether I could get there. Considering the problem from all sides, I decided that I would return to Clemson, enroll in pre-medicine, and take organic chemistry. If I passed, I would continue on the path toward a medical career; if I failed, I would do something else.

Father displayed real wisdom in guiding me into a career that has given my life so much meaning.

I tried to sign up for organic chemistry as soon as I got to the campus only to find out that I had to have a prerequisite year of analytical chemistry before I could take organic chemistry. So I signed up and took qualitative and quantitative analysis, which were not particularly hard. The following year I at long last began organic chemistry. I gave it all I had, studied very hard, and made A's both semesters, which was a great relief.

Unfortunately, I also ran into German. As a premed major, I had to have a foreign language, and someone told me that I should take German as it was the language of science. Wrong! German is not the language of science—English is. Also, German is a very difficult language for someone who is not gifted in languages, as is my case. I tried hard but never made better than mediocre to poor grades and was not held in high repute by my German professor. I remember once sitting at my desk, waiting for class to begin. I had just finished an organic chemistry class and had a returned test booklet lying on top of my books. The professor glanced down at the test booklet, noticed the grade, and said in apparent disbelief, "*You* made an A in Organic Chemistry?" (italics added to "you")

Clemson swim team, 1948

A Culinary Reason for Being an Athlete

Contrary to most colleges, the Clemson mess hall had really good food, and I loved the breaded veal cutlets that they served on rare occasions. Before long, I noticed that the training tables where the athletes ate had a different menu, which included breaded veal cutlets several times a week. That settled it! I thought about the different sports that I could go out for and decided I had the best chance of making the swimming team. I loved to swim and had always been good at it. When I first learned to swim around the age of five or six, it was like learning to fly. I was not very fast by the standards of college swimming, but I could endure. So I went out for Clemson's swimming team and made it as a 200- and 400-meter specialist.

Swimming was not highly promoted in South Carolina colleges. Most of the best swimmers went to school in other states, but Clemson was competitive in South Carolina, and I had the good fortune to win the state championship in a meet held in Columbia. When we went to meets outside the state, though, the story was something different altogether. The first time we competed with the University of Georgia in Athens, we were humiliated. The Georgia team broke seven pool records that day as I remember.

Later, we went to Gainesville, Florida, and swam against the University of Florida and several NCAA champions that were on their team. Not only were we out-manned, but our training facilities had not prepared us for the competition. In Clemson, we swam in the YMCA pool that was twenty yards long. This required many turns in swimming 220 and 440 yards. Swimmers rest on the turns, and doing all my training in a pool that size got me and all my teammates accustomed to these rests. In Florida, however, I swam in a 100-meter pool for the first time. As I swam the first lap of the 200-meter event, I remember thinking that I would never reach the end of the pool. It didn't get any better for the 400-meter event. I lost both of my events by wide margins.

Nonetheless, participating on Clemson's swimming team was one of the especially rewarding experiences of my college career.

Summers During the Clemson Years

On summer break during my Clemson years, I worked as a lifeguard and as a water-safety and swimming instructor—twice at Oconee State Park, which is in the mountains not far from Clemson, and twice at Poinsett State Park, which is in the high hills of the Santee, not far from Sumter, South Carolina. A number of interesting things happened during these summers, but probably the most important for my medical career was that at Poinsett, I met Marion Dwight, the person who would one day be my longtime partner practicing medicine in Bamberg, South Carolina.

At the time we met, I was about twenty-four, and he was ten years younger. Marion's father was superintendent of Poinsett State Park, and I became good friends with the entire family. In later years, I maintained contact with them, and after I had started my practice in Bamberg, I learned that Marion had gone to medical school and was looking for a place to begin his own career. I remembered Marion as somebody with whom I felt I could be compatible. Besides, I knew his family, and if you grow up in a small, close-knit community, as I had and as many Southerners of my generation had, you realize that family means a lot. I went down to Charleston to see a patient who was hospitalized there. I saw Marion at work in the hospital and talked him into joining me. It proved to be an excellent decision.

A few other incidents stand out from these summer jobs. One was a near accident that occurred at Oconee State Park.

When I worked at Oconee, the park superintendent would take the young people square dancing every week in Highlands, which is about twenty or thirty miles from Oconee. He would have me go with him, and I would ride in the back of the pickup, and six or seven young people would climb in the back with me. One particular night, we were coming back, and it was very cold. Fortunately, somebody had brought a blanket, so we had a blanket over everyone, and we were packed in. I was facing the rear of the truck and sat with my back against the cab of the truck, and there was a boy sitting with his back against my knees. All of a sudden I couldn't feel him pressing against my knees, so I swept down the blanket, and I said, "Don't stand up." We were driving along twisting mountain roads, and the superintendent, who liked to have a few beers while we square danced, was driving a little bit faster than he should have. Just as I said those words, I saw the boy disappear over the side of the truck. In one motion, sweeping the blanket down, I reached over the side of the truck and caught him under his armpit and flipped him back into the truck bed. I was big and strong in those days and could do such things, but even so, his feet hit the pavement for an instant, and he skinned them up. But that was all the damage that was done.

I remember the boy asking me not to tell anybody.

"My parents will never let me go anywhere again," he said, "if you say anything about what happened."

So, I said, "Okay." And I never told anybody.

One of my regular jobs at Poinsett State Park was teaching children how to swim. Since Poinsett was so close to the town of Sumter, mothers would bring carloads of children during the summer to get swimming lessons at the park. These were little children, five or six years old, and the mothers would take turns bringing all the children—seven or eight to a car—so that every mother didn't have to make the drive every day. I enjoyed seeing the children. It was a break in the day for me.

One day stands out especially in my mind. One of the usual carloads of little children pulled up at the parking lot. The driver got out and she looked just terrible. Her hair was a mess, and she looked like she had been run up one side of a hill and down another. As she came up to me, I said, "What on earth happened to you?"

"Well," she said, "when we got about halfway out here, a bee got in the car, and it just scared the children to death. That bee flew all around inside the car, and when the bee would fly to the back of the car, all the children would scream and climb into the front seat"—this was long before car seats and seat belts—"and when the bee would fly up to the front, all the children would scream and climb back into the back. And it went that way almost all the way out here."

I didn't doubt a word of what she had said, as she looked the part.

Near Poinsett was the only black state park in South Carolina—Burnt Gin State Park. This was in the late 40s, so segregation was still a fact of life in the South. One day, Mr. Dwight came to me and said, "Have you ever been in swimming with black people?"

"No, sir," I answered.

"Well," he said, "they want you to go to Burnt Gin and certify the lifeguard out there."

I said that was fine with me.

So I went over to Burnt Gin and gave the course to the black lifeguard and certified him. I didn't attach much significance to this chore at the time. After all, I was the head lifeguard and the appropriate person for Mr. Dwight to ask to go. But the truth is, the majority of white people would have turned down Mr. Dwight. I think, though, he knew me well enough to be confident that I would accept the task, do a good job, and do it without reservation.

Acceptance to Medical School

After three years at Clemson, I had completed all the requirements for admission to medical school, but I had not taken some of the preparatory courses that would serve as introductions to the same courses at medical school, among those were embryology and histology.

Nevertheless, I was encouraged to apply for medical school during my third year at Clemson. There was fierce competition for admission, as this was the peak period when veterans were graduating from college. We heard that there were 3,000 total applicants and over 600 in-state applicants for the 60 vacancies for our class at the Medical College of the State of South Carolina (now the Medical University of South Carolina). No out-of-state applicants were accepted at that time. The large number of in-state applicants reflected the surge of veterans who had come into the educational system at that time.

The best strategy, therefore, was thought to be to apply during your third year and then apply again in your fourth year, as many students were accepted only after they had applied two or three times. I took the Medical College Aptitude Test (MEDCAP) in the spring of my third year and sent in my application. This was a new test and had never been offered before. I didn't think it was particularly difficult.

As part of the application process, I had to get a letter of recommendation from a faculty member, so I presented myself to the dean of the school and asked that he give me one. I remember he looked over my record and said, in a gruff voice, "Well, if you are not mature now, you never will be."

When I received a letter of acceptance on this, my first try, I had some misgivings about the wisdom of the admissions committee at the Medical College of the State of South Carolina. On the other hand, I was proud to have been accepted after only three years of college, even though I had never expected to be. Throughout my first few weeks of medical school, I was more than a little intimidated and continued to worry about how I could compete with those students who had completed the preparatory courses that I had never taken.

At the time I was accepted for medical school, I had not yet earned my undergraduate degree, but Clemson had a policy at that time that those who left after three years and graduated from medical school could apply for and receive their undergraduate degree upon graduation from medical school. Therefore, when I was graduating from medical school in the spring of 1953, I wrote Clemson and requested that my Clemson diploma be mailed to me. I got a letter in return stating that I had to come to the graduation exercise in order to receive the degree. So a few days after receiving my doctoral degree, I walked across the stage at Clemson wearing my doctoral gown and hood to receive my B.S. degree. Furthermore, I was put in their records as having graduated in 1953, which meant that for several years I received alumni news about the class of '53 even though I didn't know a single person in it. Later they transferred my name to the class of 1949, which was the year that I left Clemson.

All of that, of course, was far in the future. In 1949, my primary concern was doing my very best in medical school, and my first challenge in that respect was finding out when exactly my training would start. In those days, the Medical College of the

State of South Carolina sent only a letter of acceptance. They did not send any schedule, not even a notice of when classes would begin. By asking a current medical student who lived in a town near Ridge Spring, I found out that the first day of class was always on the same day, something like "the Thursday after the second Sunday in August." During the summer of 1949, I made my plans to move to Charleston, South Carolina, for the beginning of my medical training.

Medical College

MEDICAL SCHOOL

I arrived in Charleston to attend the Medical College of the State of South Carolina in August of 1949. The campus of the Medical College was very simple. One building housed the library, all the lab space, the lecture hall, and the auditorium. This seems unbelievable until you realize that the building was used only for the first two years of schooling, during which we studied the basic sciences. Each class met in a single body and had the same schedule. It was a far cry from the present complex of the Medical University of South Carolina.

Old Charleston and Mrs. Wilkins's Boarding House

After checking in at the school, I still needed a place to live, and the registrar directed me to a house on Smith Street, within easy walking distance of the Medical College. This was a good thing, as I did not own a car. The owner of the house was Mrs. Bessie Wilkins, an older lady and a genial hostess who operated an old-fashioned boarding house. Not only did she let out rooms, she also prepared all the meals (with the help of a black woman) and served them family-style at a set hour each day.

Mrs. Wilkins had been reared in the Charleston area, perhaps on the Sea Islands—the sandy, low-lying barrier islands along South Carolina's coast—and had a thick Charleston brogue. In addition to Mrs. Wilkins and the tenants, the household included

Mrs. Wilkins' daughter and son-in-law and an old black man who lived in one of the back rooms and helped with the chores. I understood that Mr. Wilkins had died some years before.

The house was a wood-framed structure, reminiscent of another century. There was a foyer inside the front door and a stairway leading to the second floor where there were four bedrooms, each having a Dutch door opening onto the hall. Like most of the older housing in Charleston, this house was designed for maximum relief from the heat in the long hot summers with little thought about the occasional cold snap that sometimes occurred in winter. The heat for the downstairs and the bedrooms came from a large, freestanding oil stove called a Heatroller. Hot air rose from the Heatroller into the upper hallway and then filtered into each bedroom. In its day, Mrs. Wilkins's home was a nice middle-class dwelling.

Besides paying for my tuition, the GI Bill also paid me $52 a month for living expenses, which was enough to get by but not enough to pay for a room of my own. Like many other medical students, therefore, I was happy to share a room with another student. My roommate was a first-year medical student named Jim Connor. He was from Walterboro, South Carolina, and I met him for the first time at Mrs. Wilkins's home. I didn't know it then, but Jim and I would share many hours of study and hard work over the next several years. Jim was also a Clemson graduate, but I had not known him there. Although he was younger, he had been in the class ahead of me. But since he had graduated after four years and I had left after three, we reached medical school the same year.

Next door to Mrs. Wilkins' was a rooming house that did not serve meals. Three of my soon-to-be classmates—Bill Freeman, Hubert Smoak, and Bill Dukes—lived there, but they took their meals with us.

Charleston was, and is, a very historic city, but in the early 1950s, its past glory was really in the past, and there was almost no sign of affluence. Even the Battery, the most exclusive and aristocratic neighborhood in the city, showed signs of deterioration, and other Charlestonians said of those who lived on the Battery, they were "too poor to paint and too proud to whitewash."

This was my first visit to Charleston, and I would like to have looked all around the city. My time, however, was almost completely taken up with my studies, and I never did get to see as much of Charleston as I would have liked. There is an old saying that "medicine is a jealous mistress," and beginning in medical school, I found that to be true. If I had not had the experience of the Marine Corps and learned discipline from that, I doubt that I could have met the demands of medical school, particularly the demand for total commitment. Over the next few years, one of my friends who had a car would occasionally invite me to ride around the town. As I rode around, though, I found myself spending much of my time envying the people who were standing on the street corners with nothing to do, or so it seemed, while I was eternally behind schedule.

Classes Begin

On the first day of classes, all sixty students in the class of 1953 assembled for orientation in Baruch Auditorium. Each class had sixty students, and all of the medical students—fifty-eight males and two females in our class—had the same class schedule. The dean got up and talked for a few minutes on nothing in particular and finished by saying, "Directly above us is the anatomy lab. You will assemble there in ten minutes."

That was it for orientation.

Going into the anatomy lab was something all of us had dreaded. After all, most of us had never seen a dead body, and in this place not only would there be dead bodies, but we would be required to dissect them.

The anatomy lab was a large room with fifteen tables upon which lay fifteen draped cadavers. The faculty was very business-like, and without further ado divided us into fifteen groups of four, assigned us to a table and a cadaver. We had all brought dissecting instruments as we had been instructed, but our first chore was to bathe the cadaver and shave all the hair off. After the first touch, we became less anxious, as we had something to do.

Cadaver Problems

Four of us—Charley White, Jim Connor, Julius Earle, and I—made up one team. The cadavers were unclaimed bodies from state institutions, mostly from the State Hospital, but ours was from the penitentiary. He was a huge black male who had been electrocuted, and because he was somewhat obese, dissection became more of a chore, as all the fat must be removed and discarded in order to expose and identify the other structures.

After about two weeks, though, another fact about our cadaver became obvious. It seems that the electrocution had damaged the circulation and interfered with the embalming process. The anatomy lab was not air-conditioned, and August in Charleston is sweltering and steamy. Soon it became obvious that our cadaver had a particularly offensive odor that none of the others had. This odor traveled home with us, much to the dismay of Mrs. Wilkins and our fellow boarders. Nonetheless, our complaints to the faculty fell on deaf ears at first. But as the odor took on a nauseating quality, everyone in the anatomy lab, including the faculty, began to complain, and we were given a replacement. The fact that our team was now behind with our work and had to start over seemed of little concern to the faculty. It was simply one of the challenges that we, as medical students, were expected to overcome.

Our second cadaver was from the State Hospital and had suffered a stroke, which, unfortunately, left one side atrophied and made the cadaver less than desirable as a study object, but at least he was thin.

Dr. O'Driscoll—Anatomy

One member of the anatomy faculty was a gruff, bluff man named Dr. Cyrus "Cy" O'Driscoll. He was long past retirement age, but he continued to teach, as he loved human anatomy. Dr. O'Driscoll smoked a pipe constantly, and it was his habit to walk around the lab explaining fine details of the anatomical area under study. As he talked, the pipe remained in his mouth, and saliva ran down the pipe stem to the bowl and then dripped off onto the cadaver. Sometimes he would become so engrossed in what he was saying, he would remove the pipe from his mouth and lay it on the cadaver's chest. When he had finished, he picked up the pipe and returned it to his mouth.

Dr. O'Driscoll had spent his whole professional life in the anatomy lab and was sometimes called to testify in court as an expert witness. Once, after giving his opinion on some anatomical question, one of the attorneys asked, "What is your authority for that answer?" Quick as a wink, Dr. O'Driscoll drew himself up in the full pride of his profession and replied, "Over ten thousand dead bodies, Sir!"

On the first day of anatomy class, a list of texts was written on the blackboard, and we were told that we were responsible for any fact that was in any of these books, plus details from Dr. O'Driscoll's drawings. It seemed that over the years, he had discovered anatomical minutiae that were in no published text. For each region of the body under study, Dr. O'Driscoll had a set of his hand-done drawings, which he would post everywhere in the lab by taping them to the walls and the large columns that supported the ceiling. None of the other faculty tested us on these drawings, but Dr. O'Driscoll always did. As we didn't know who was going to test us until we came into the lab, we always had to learn Dr. O'Driscoll's drawings as well as the material in the regular texts.

The method of testing was different from anything any of us had ever experienced. Each time we finished studying a region of the body, four students were assigned to one faculty member, who would then test that group for two hours, orally. The first hour took place in a classroom and was divided into fifteen minutes per student, with questions that could be general, such as, "Tell me all you know about the brachial plexus," or specific, such as, "Name the muscles of the forearm, their origin and insertion, blood supply, innervation, and function." After this hour, the group would move into the lab to the dissection table. There each student would have fifteen minutes of identifying various structures upon command. The student might be asked to pick up a certain structure, such as a muscle, or he might be asked to trace the course of an artery, vein, or nerve, showing its branches, their names, and what structures it supplied.

Dr. O'Driscoll added his own special touch to this pressure cooker. He had a large "Big Ben" alarm clock that he used in his testing. He would say, for instance, "Name the foramina"— holes — "of the skull and tell what passes through each one." Then he would set his Big Ben for the number of minutes that he felt the answer required. The Big Ben was a good eight inches in diameter and made a very loud tick. In the silence that often followed as the student collected his thoughts, the tick of that clock only heightened the sense of anxiety that filled the room. This was particularly true if the student drew a blank and could not think of anything to say. In this situation, or if the student gave what Dr. O'Driscoll considered an inadequate answer, the professor would turn to the next student and say, "You answer that. He didn't even know enough to ruin it!"

On one occasion, I walked into class prepared to take the scheduled exam. But when the testing was about to begin, a great cry went up from the majority of the class, who, for some reason, had not gotten the word about the test. In a rare display of human kindness, the faculty agreed to put off the test. Unfortunately, this was one time that I didn't want such kindness. I felt that I had peaked and was ready for the test. I wanted to get it behind me. So I asked if those who were prepared could take it. After talking it over among themselves, the faculty agreed that if four students wanted to take it then, they would be tested. I found three other students and reported that we were ready.

We were assigned to Dr. O'Driscoll who proceeded to test us not for two but for four hours. Apparently he had nothing else to do. You would have thought that after more than two years in the marines, I would have learned the pitfalls of volunteering for anything.

On a typical testing day, the oral examination lasted an hour. But on this particular day, it went on for two hours, with Dr. O'Driscoll's Big Ben ticking away the whole time. Then we moved into the lab for the practical exam.

As he grilled us on the minutiae of the cadaver's anatomy, he held a clipboard close to his chest and recorded our grades. We soon found that if we stood behind him and a little to the right, when he let the clipboard down slightly to record a grade, we could see the grades we were getting. Unfortunately, it didn't take us long to realize that he had us hopelessly confused and no one was getting the grade he deserved. Some of us were ecstatic and others glum as he continued recording good grades and bad, but giving credit to the wrong students.

Studying the Human Skeleton

The first six weeks of gross anatomy was devoted to osteology, a study of the bones, and each of us was given a portion of a human skeleton to aid us in our study. I remember the first night Jim and I studied with our "bag of bones," as it was called. We sat down after supper with the bones and Grey's Anatomy. We were to memorize the name of each bone, how it got the name, the features of each bone, its physical description, all its borders and surfaces, the areas where muscles attach, the names of the foramina where nerves and blood vessels pierce it, and its articulating surfaces where it forms a joint with another bone. All of these, and probably more, have names. Our first bone was the clavicle, whose name comes from the Latin word for "key," which it was thought to resemble. It has twenty-one borders and surfaces. At about 11 PM, we were still trying to remember the names of all of these and had not even started on its other features nor on any other bone. Jim suddenly looked at me with real tears in his eyes and said, "Mike, if I had known it was going to be this hard, I wouldn't have come."

In short order, we dropped into a pattern of studying from after supper until early in the morning, sometimes surviving on only one or two hours of sleep, if that much. On the weekends we slept a little more—sometimes.

(I should note here that despite his momentary fears, Jim did well in his studies, graduated, and pursued a career in pediatrics. He retired from teaching Infectious Disease in the University of California, San Diego Medical School. We still keep in contact and occasionally visit each other.)

Facial Muscles After Midnight

One night, Jim and I began studying the muscles of the face—name, origin and insertion, blood supply, nerve supply, and function. As one described a muscle, the other, holding the book, would correct the description and demonstrate this by flexing that muscle in his face. By midnight, we still had a long way to go, but the demonstrations of the muscular functions had become comic routines of the first order. After each demonstration, we would erupt in hysterical laughter and then, somehow, try to get back to the serious business at hand. This effort of alternating laughter and seriousness went on through the night, and we did not finally crawl into bed until about 5 AM.

Unknown to us, several executives from Armour & Co.—the company that Mrs. Wilkins's son-in-law worked for—were visiting from out of town, and the Wilkins had invited them to stay in the room next to ours. In the morning, we both got an earful from the Wilkins family, as their guests had not slept a wink and were wondering what kinds of idiots Mrs. Wilkins allowed to stay in her house.

Dr. Melvin Knisely—Histology

Dr. Melvin Knisely was the chairman of the anatomy department. He had come to Charleston a year or two before and was a nationally-known figure, as he had discovered "sludged blood" and had been covered in a multi-page article in Life magazine. He also taught two lectures in histology, which is the study of minute anatomical tissue through the use of microscopes. In one, he said that looking through a microscope is like flying over country in an airplane. In the other, he said, "Histology is the science of repeatable artifact." Referring to the box of slides that each of us was given at the start of the histology course, he told us that what we were looking at under the microscope was nothing at all like the tissues actually were, but had been processed in such a way as to make the same errors and distortions each time. He illustrated this point by likening it to an airplane flying over an area at a great height. He pointed out that the patchwork we would see from the plane would be nothing like the view we would get at ground level. So too with the slides.

On the day of the final exam in histology, we entered the room to find a single slide at each of our desks. At a signal, we had one minute to put this slide under our microscope, identify the tissue, write down the answer on an answer sheet, and pass the slide to the person on our right. There was a signal every minute for one hour, and then we were finished with the practical part of the exam.

Next came the written part, which consisted of only five questions, of which I remember only the first one: "Write all you know about the liver." The other questions were similarly broad. Books had been written about each of the five questions, and I suspected our answers would never be more than scanned, but I was too fearful not to answer them as fully as I could. It took me more than five hours to complete the written part of the exam.

Dr. Elsie Tabor—Embryology

One of the things that I was most apprehensive about in coming to medical school from my third year at Clemson was that I had not had a course in embryology. I hardly knew what the word meant, and all my classmates were unanimous in their descriptions of how hard it was.

Adding to my misery were the stories that were told about the embryology professor, Dr. Elsie Tabor. Her lectures were demanding and full of information that was swiftly presented. As she lectured, she drew complex drawings of fetal growth on the blackboard. Moving along the blackboard, she lectured very rapidly, drawing with her right hand and erasing with her left as she moved along. It was astonishing and intimidating, but following the advice of the upperclassmen, we quickly found that we could survive by working in pairs—one to copy the drawings and the other to take notes on what she said.

After my first lecture with Dr. Tabor, however, I was no longer worried that I had not taken the embryology course in undergraduate school. At Clemson, the course had covered embryology up to the development of a 10-mm. pig embryo. That is exactly what we covered in Dr. Tabor's first session. After that, we were all even.

Dr. Tabor was a no-nonsense person in class, and we respected her highly. After completing her course, however, we found that she was also a warm person who became good friends with all of us. She continued her interest in her students throughout their stay in medical school and beyond.

Mr. Anliker—Neuroanatomy

Neuroanatomy was taught by Mr. Anliker, my only teacher with only a master's degree. The rest had at least one doctorate. He, along with several others on the anatomy faculty, had been brought from Chicago by Dr. Knisely as his hand-picked research team. Unfortunately, their skills tended more toward research than teaching, and they came across as a peculiar bunch with their thoughts lost in the lofty clouds of research. Mr. Anliker was the strangest one of all. Prior to coming to Charleston, he had never owned a car, but cars were a necessity in Charleston due to the lack of public transportation, so he bought one. Several years later, his car wouldn't start, so he called a mechanic, who discovered that Mr. Anliker had never done a thing to maintain the car other than having the gas tank filled periodically. He had never checked the oil, and the poor old engine, with its moving parts unlubricated for years, had run as long as it could, but now, dry as a bone, it had frozen up and would never run again.

Mr. Anliker's lectures were almost as dry as his car's engine, but in his defense, he had a dry subject.

Dr. Whip McCord—Biochemistry

Dr. William M. "Whip" McCord taught biochemistry and was a superb teacher. He later went on to be a fine president of the medical school. His lectures were concise, interesting, and well-presented. He had an interesting way of emphasizing a point that he wanted to get across. He would repeat a sentence or phrase over and over at the beginning of the class. I remember in a lecture on nutrition he kept repeating, "Ice cream and cake are good foods. Ice cream and cake are good foods." He must have said it fifteen times. His point was that some things are bad only in excessive amounts.

Dr. Theodore Bernthal—Physiology

Dr. Theodore Bernthal was the head of the physiology department, besides being a lecturer. He was also a stickler for details. One of the assistant professors once said of him, "Dr. Bernthal does everything the hard way. He probably conceived his children standing in a hammock."

He opened his first lecture by saying, "In every subject that you have studied, the professor has thought that his subject was the most important one that you will study in preparation for your career. But I am ready to tell you right now that physiology *is* the most important course you will take in medical school." He was deadly serious.

Dr. Kinard's Advice

For me, physiology was especially interesting, because it was in this course that we learned how the different organs and tissues of the body functioned. One organ that captured my particular interest was the pancreas. It was little understood at that time, and I became quite caught up in studying its marvelous intricacies. At one point, I became quite excited when I thought I had discovered a new way to study one of its functions. Flushed with insight, I went to Dr. Kinard, another department staff member who was highly regarded by the students. He had a PhD in physiology as well as an MD, a dual achievement that was rare in those days. Dr. Kinard was a retiring person but also kind and thoroughly approachable. He listened patiently as I explained my ideas and then startled me with his reply. He said, "Do you want to be a physician and help sick people?"

"Yes, sir," I answered.

"Then you forget about this right now!" he said.

I was stunned. I couldn't understand why a man of his background wouldn't encourage me to pursue a higher level of scientific knowledge. But I was a conscientious young man, so I replied, "Yes, sir."

Then I turned away, thoroughly rebuffed.

Although I will never know exactly why Dr. Kinard gave such an adamant response, I eventually came to believe that at one time, he had probably been the same sort of enthusiastic student that I was. Like me, he had probably gotten caught up in research, and that had caused him to change his objectives. Now he was stuck in a career that was not what he had intended. Unfortunately, no one gave him the advice he gave me, and I have always been profoundly grateful to him.

A Cold and Fruitless Thanksgiving Holiday

One of the demanding aspects of physiology was that we were required to hand in typed reports of physiology experiments. It didn't take me long to realize that I could not afford to pay for this service, so I decided that I would have to type my own reports despite the fact that I had never had a day of typing instruction. For $75, I bought a portable typewriter from another student and just began to type. A book of instruction came with it, but as the reports had to be turned in weekly, I decided I could not afford the luxury of learning the traditional manner of typing. So I taught myself the two-finger hunt-and-peck method, which I continue to use to this day, although I now use a computer instead of a typewriter. I have developed some speed with this method, as long as I am writing my own material from my head. When I copy material written by others, my speed drops precipitously.

When Thanksgiving holidays of my second year came around, I decided I could not afford to take any time away from my studies, so instead of going home, I decided I would stay in Charleston and catch up on my typing. It wasn't that I couldn't have gone home. Although I had no car, Bob Owen, a student in the school of pharmacy, was from Batesburg, just a few miles from my hometown of Ridge Spring, and he would have been glad to give me a ride home. But I was determined to be productive and so turned Bob down when he offered me a lift.

On the Wednesday night before Thanksgiving, the man who was boarding in the room across the hall came in after drinking too much, shoved open both his windows as high as they would go (it being a mild evening), and passed out on his bed. About 3 AM, I woke up, freezing cold. My teeth were chattering, and my whole body shivered. It turned out that while everyone in the house and throughout Charleston was sleeping soundly in their beds, a record-breaking and unanticipated cold wave had come through and dropped the temperature into the low teens.

There was no way to get warm, as the Heatroller, our only source of heat was a poor heater at best and no match for this kind of cold, especially with all the hot air that it generated going up the stairwell and out the open windows. There was not a warm room in the house. Worst of all, as I was stiff all over from the cold, my fingers were not flexible enough to type, so I spent a cold, miserable Thanksgiving holiday, unable to do any of the work I had planned and tried to stay warm by huddling under the covers of my bed (as was everybody else in the house), and wishing I had gone home.

Dr. Benjamin Boltjes and Gas Gangrene

Dr. Benjamin Boltjes was the professor of bacteriology. He was a giant of a man and had no foolishness about him or in his classroom or lab. In donating blood, he always gave a pint and a half because that was his opinion of himself.

One day, we went into the bacteriology lab and were slapped in the face with the worst odor that any of us had ever experienced—a pungent, nauseating smell, worse even than my original putrefying cadaver. We soon found its source—a dead rabbit on one of the tables. It seems that Dr. Boltjes had inoculated the rabbit with the bacteria that causes gas gangrene, and when the gangrene was at its peak, the rabbit was sacrificed, brought to the lab, and left there while we worked for the next three hours. Dr. Boltjes wanted to be sure we could recognize this indicator of gas gangrene under any circumstances.

Apparently it worked. For thirty years later, as I was walking down a hall at Bamberg County Memorial Hospital, I smelled the odor again for the first time since Dr. Boltjes's class. Without hesitating, I turned to the nurse with me and asked, "Who has gas gangrene?"

She was thunderstruck, as there was indeed a patient being treated for gas gangrene, but he was being treated by another doctor, and she had no idea where I had gotten my information. Merely walking past the patient's room was all I needed to bring back an old, well-learned lesson.

The Long Line for Grades

One thing about the first year of medical school that, to this day, I feel was unnecessarily harsh and stressful was that no grades were given until the last day of the year. Imagine going through nine months of intense study and periodic examinations without a clue as to how you were doing. All of the students were very bright, and I think most of us were more than a little intimidated by our competition. It seemed unfair to leave us hanging in suspense and giving us no clue as to how well we were progressing.

On the last day of the year, we stood in line in alphabetical order and one by one filed by the registrar and were handed an envelope with our grades inside. We were instructed to open the envelope and read the report inside. If we had any questions, we were to ask them at that time. If we had no questions, we were excused and could leave.

Needless to say, there were quite a few pale faces in that lineup, and I recall one young man, who went on to become a fine surgeon, vomiting from the stress of the situation. Being near the tail-end of this alphabetical assembly, I had quite a while to contemplate my fate. I sustained myself by repeating, over and over, "They aren't going to kill me. I just might not be a doctor."

Two Years of Clinical Work

The four years of medical school were divided into two years of basic sciences and then two years of clinical work with patients. We all breathed a sigh of relief when we successfully passed the first two years, as we were told that no one ever flunked the clinic years.

Medical College of South Carolina, Class of 1953

Old Roper Hospital

I did most of my clinical training at "Old" Roper Hospital, the charity hospital for Charleston County. The building was so old it still had "pneumonia porches" on the front, which remained from the days when the major treatment for pneumonia was fresh air.

The first two floors consisted of several 60-bed wards divided as to condition treated (medicine, surgery, pediatrics, and obstetrics), sex, and race, although I don't recall ever seeing a white patient in the hospital. On the third floor, black private patients were treated by their private physicians, but we students were not allowed to go there.

Conditions were somewhat grim. I remember sitting on a patient's bed and taking an exhaustive medical history, which took several hours. At one point, I looked down and saw a large rat scurry by my foot. Quickly, I stamped down and killed it.

Old Roper has long since been torn down.

Each of the two years of clinical training was divided into quarters, and the class itself was divided into quarters. Each quarter concentrated on one of the major specialties—medicine, surgery, obstetrics, and pediatrics. Each quarter there would be a shift, and the students in each specialty would move to another specialty.

Each specialty required us to do histories and physicals, but the required history and physical were different for each specialty. Medicine's was the worst one. The history was about eight single-spaced typewritten pages of questions and answers. It often took four or five hours to complete. The purpose was to make us as familiar as possible with the symptoms of many diseases. Looking back, I can say that those hours spent preparing histories were well worth the effort, as experience has taught me that 85 to 90 percent of all diagnoses can be made from history alone, although the accuracy of the diagnosis often must be confirmed by physical examination and other tests.

When the shift came each quarter, each student would have to repeat the entire history and physical that had already been done by his predecessor.

The Palpable Gall Bladder

When I rotated onto the medical floor during my third year, I inherited several patients whose treatment was in progress; nevertheless, I had to do a long-form history and physical on them. One of the patients was a heavily jaundiced middle-aged black male with the diagnosis of hepatitis. As I was doing the physical examination, I felt a mass in the right upper quadrant of his abdomen. The more I felt it, the more certain I became that the mass was indeed there and that it was most probably his gall bladder. At that stage of my training, I did not know the significance of a palpable gall bladder in a jaundiced patient—that it almost certainly indicated cancer of the head of the pancreas, which would cause obstruction of the bile duct. I did, however, know that I shouldn't be able to feel this patient's gall bladder unless something was wrong.

So I called to my friend Bill Miller, who happened by, and asked him to examine my patient's abdomen. He too thought he felt the gall bladder. I went over to the desk and told the medicine resident that we could feel the patient's gall bladder. He immediately stopped what he was doing, came over and examined the patient. "No," he said. "I don't feel any gall bladder." And with that, he sat down and resumed his work.

Bill and I walked back, re-examined the patient, and were sure we could feel it. We asked several other people who came by to examine him, but nobody else felt the gall bladder. Nonetheless, I felt certain of my findings, so I put a notice on the wall by the patient's bed, asking other students and doctors to see what they found. On the notice, I included two columns—one for those who believed they could feel the gall bladder and one for those who did not. After a day or two, there were ten or twelve signatures in the "nay" column and only Bill and mine in the "yea" column.

In those days, probably the leading clinician in the school was Dr. Vince Moseley. He came by, read the notice, and examined the patient's abdomen. Without a word, he added his name to the column of those who *did* feel the gall bladder.

Within twenty-four hours, arrows were drawn from every signature in the nay column over to the yea column. The patient was transferred to the surgical service, had exploratory surgery, and was found to have cancer of the head of the pancreas.

This physical finding was of extreme importance, as cancer of the head of the pancreas is a "silent tumor" and very difficult to diagnose in the early stages. The cancer will obstruct the bile duct leading from the gall bladder to the small bowel. Obstruction of this duct will lead to the slow distention of the gall bladder.

I have occasionally wondered whether the gall bladder incident had anything to do with my making an "A" in medicine that year.

The Patient Who Had Been a Slave

One of the patients I had while I was a third-year student was a black man who was around a hundred years old. He was totally deaf and had been for years. He was from one of the Sea Islands, and I don't remember what his primary diagnosis was. However, as I was doing the physical examination, I was unable to examine his ear drum because his ear canal was tightly occluded with cerumen (earwax). In fact, it was the worst such occlusion I had ever seen. The wax was as hard as stone, and I know that my removing it must have been painful for the old man, but he gave no indication that it hurt. In fact, he made almost no sound at all. Finally, after about fifteen minutes (which seemed like two hours) and some bleeding, I cleared both canals and could see a normal ear drum on each side.

With the clearing, a marvelous change came over the old man. He began to talk—in volumes. He told me about life during "slavery times" when he was a little boy. He did not know how old he was, but he believed that he was about six or seven years of age when "freedom came." He told me that he had lived on a plantation whose master had a boat that was paddled to and from Charleston with passengers and commercial cargo.

His mind was bright and clear, and the hospital nurses and aides were fascinated. I called a reporter from a Charleston newspaper who interviewed him and wrote an article. While he was on the ward, I felt like I was living with a part of history. But then he got well and left the hospital, and I never saw him again.

The Excised Umbilicus

When we were in our final year and on the surgical service, a lot of each student's time was spent at "New" Roper Hospital, assisting the surgeons as they operated on their private patients. Once I was there assisting with a case involving an abdominal operation. The surgeon was a very precise and meticulous person who always insisted on everything being just right. When the patient was asleep, he and the first assistant began preparing the skin of the abdomen for the surgery by scrubbing it with a variety of cleaning agents. As he was preparing the umbilicus (the belly button), he began to talk about what a vile and useless thing this was, how it was impossible to clean and how it frequently caused infections. As he talked, he got more and more worked up, but he continued to prepare the patient for surgery.

When he finished draping the patient, he took the scalpel and began a midline incision from the top of the abdomen down almost to the pubic bone, carefully going around the umbilicus. Then, instead of going to the next step of the surgery, he went back and made another incision around the other side of the umbilicus, excised it, and threw it into the trashcan. I was thunderstruck. I had never seen or heard of anything being done like this. Being a mere medical student, however, I made no objection to the surgeon's action.

Two days later, as I was sitting at the desk at the nurses' station writing a progress note on this same patient's chart, a student nurse that I knew came along, and I began telling her about the patient and how the surgeon had excised his umbilicus and thrown it into the trash can, which led us into a detailed discussion of the difficulty of living without an umbilicus. (For instance, where would you put the salt when you ate celery in bed, etc.) The more we talked, the more tickled we became. We began tossing out wilder and funnier illustrations, laughing almost uncontrollably and thinking ourselves quite the clever pair.

Finally, when we had gotten some control over ourselves, I got up to leave, as I had more work to do, but when I turned around, I saw the patient's wife sitting about five feet from where this insensitive and unprofessional conversation had just taken place. I'm sure that my face turned several shades of red, but I walked right by the woman and very studiously never asked about her husband. I and my friend, I'm sure, learned a valuable lesson that day. The only way to deal with loose language that would be better off not having been said is not to say it. It can never be taken back.

South Carolina State Hospital

In our third year at medical school, we were all required to go to Columbia and spend a week at South Carolina State Hospital, the hospital for the mentally ill.

This was before the advent of the multitude of drugs that we now use to treat mental illness, especially schizophrenia. Very little effective treatment was available, and patients were committed, often for the balance of their lives, to the state hospital to protect themselves and others. The magnitude of the problem was evidenced by the fact that, at that time, of the 10,000 hospital beds in the state, approximately 5,000 of them were occupied by patients suffering from schizophrenia.

The state hospital was a world unto itself. Conditions were very basic. The patients were housed in large wards of either forty or sixty beds, and everything was under lock and key. It was here that I first witnessed electroconvulsive therapy (ECT)—otherwise known as shock therapy—a treatment that became popular in the 1930s and 1940s and was sometimes abused in state hospital settings.

ECT is given by placing an electrode on either side of the patient's head and sending an electric charge into the electrodes. This is invariably accompanied by a generalized seizure that lasts only a few seconds and is followed by a postictal state, a period of deep unconsciousness that lasts for a period of several minutes followed by a brief period of confusion. This treatment, highly refined, is still the most effective treatment for emotional depression but has little value for anything else, to my knowledge. Today, the patient is deeply, briefly sedated and given a paralytic agent.

ECT is then given, the patient doesn't move a muscle and has no recollection of the experience when awakened.

This refined form of the therapy was not what I witnessed in 1951.

I remember the incident as if it were yesterday. I accompanied a psychiatrist into one of the large wards. The ward had been prepared by taking most of the mattresses off the single beds where the patients slept and putting them on the floor beside each bed. An attendant had brought in a plain wooden table with a top that was padded, and the ECT generator was placed on its own small table.

These sessions were held three days a week, so the patients were well aware of what was to take place. When we entered the ward, the patients crowded around the table to watch. About six of the largest and strongest patients were selected to assist with the procedure.

As I watched, the psychiatrist read a name from a list that he was carrying. Immediately, one of the assistants grabbed the patient, and the others wrestled him to the table and laid him down on it. Another assistant placed the electrodes on the patient's head, the psychiatrist activated the generator, and the patient had a seizure followed by postictal unconsciousness. He was then picked up, carried to a mattress, and laid on it by the assistants. The mattresses were put on the floor to prevent injury, as the patient would awake in a confused state and might fall to the floor.

The procedure was repeated over and over until there were no more names on the list. Occasionally, the name of one of the assistants was called, and the other assistants would turn on him and wrestle him to the table—to the great glee of the onlookers.

After my week at this facility, I came away thinking, *This is a hospital?*

Fortunately, we have come a long way in our care of these, often-tragic people, but we still have a long way to go. We have wonderful drugs—with more in the process of development—that will often restore these patients to a functional state, *as long as they take the medication!* In short, we have drugs that will control the symptoms of the illness, but few if any cures.

When these drugs were first introduced, there followed a great wave of enthusiasm to empty the state hospitals, and occupancy was reduced by more than 90 percent. The patients were given the new drugs until they were back to an adequately functional state and released to local mental health facilities, which were ill-equipped to receive them, as there was no intensive case management system in place—and still isn't. By that I mean that the patients, who are treated as outpatients, receive good treatment as long as they return to the clinic on a regular schedule and continue to take their medications. If they don't continue to take the medications, the original problem recurs, and they are back in society without means of help. The result is that an estimated 80 to 90 percent of our homeless persons are graduates of the mental health system who have been lost to follow-up. The obvious answer is to develop new and curative drugs or, short of that, to provide intensive case management that will provide mental health workers to find patients who fail to return for their appointments to make sure they take their medication. The obvious problem with this remedy is that it would be frightfully expensive.

What a shame that the richest nation on earth, a nation that can send rockets to the moon, virtually abandons hundreds of thousands of its ill and helpless citizens to a life on the streets.

Servant to the Poor

Much of my clinical work was done with indigent patients at Old Roper and in the clinics at the Medical College. An experience in one of those clinics burned itself into my memory and probably had something to do with the commitment to service that I made later in my life.

The Vascular Clinic was called the boot clinic by the junior medical students and was developed to treat those indigent patients who had ischemic leg ulcers. These ulcers that were due to poor circulation in the lower extremities and this basic problem of circulatory insufficiency were beyond the curative power of medicine at the time. The treatment, which rarely cured the ulcer but simply delayed its progression, was to apply an Unna's paste boot. This involved painting a paste containing a mixture of gelatin and zinc oxide on the leg, then wrapping a layer of gauze over this, then painting again. These layers were alternated until a "boot" of about four alternating layers was formed. The gelatin kept it soft and flexible, and it was quite comfortable. It also absorbed most of the drainage from the ulcer. The patients were scheduled to return monthly to have the boot replaced with fresh gauze and zinc oxide.

The patients came into the clinic and were assigned to a student in rotation. The month-old boot was usually very dirty and in poor condition. First, the old boot was cut away with scissors and the ulcer exposed. In the warmer months, it was not uncommon to find maggots in the ulcer. (This was a disgusting sight and slightly nauseating early in the students' experience. But the maggots served a useful purpose by removing the necrotic and devitalized tissue. In the earlier days of medicine, this was recognized as helpful, and maggots were put in wounds to clean them out. Our professors, however, were thoroughly modern and instructed us to remove maggots whenever found.) After this, the entire foot and leg, ulcer and all were bathed and cleaned, as they had not been bathed for a month, at least. Then the boot was reapplied.

This was a profound experience for me, as my only contact in the past with persons of this social stratum was one in which they had been, in one way or another, servants to me. Now I was being given the opportunity to be their servant. The implications of washing their feet, from a Christian perspective, were not lost on my conscience so that even at this early stage in my medical career, I began growing sensitive to the needs of the poor and my role in serving them.

Enjoying summer internship in Los Angeles

Summer Internship in Los Angeles

In the summer interim between my third and fourth years of medical school, two of my friends, Hubert Smoak and Bill Freeman, invited me to go with them to California to work in the Methodist Hospital in Los Angeles. Hubert had a car, we could split the gasoline expense, and each pay for his own lodging and meals. I had spent the previous summers, while at Clemson and medical school, working as a lifeguard at state parks just to earn money. I was worn out with that, and this offered me a chance to gain helpful experience at a cost that I could afford, as the hospital was going to pay us a small salary. I also figured I could sell blood if I needed more money. (This was a common way for medical students to make money, as there were no national programs of blood banks for collecting and distributing blood.)

So we left in the early summer and drove the distance in three or four days with an occasional brief stop to visit spots of interest. Hubert and Bill planned our itinerary and did most of the driving. I spent my time learning to play a concertina that I had bought.

The only other time I had seen the West was from a troop train on my way home from the Pacific after the war, so I found special enjoyment on this trip and saw many beautiful places and spectacular scenery, but the Grand Canyon topped them all. The air was like crystal and the distances so vast that it seemed like a painting. I can remember it clearly to this day.

When we arrived at the hospital, we were shown our rooms and treated as if we were graduates. Our title was "Extern." We spent one weekend in San Francisco, just looking around, but since I had not planned on this extra expense, I sold a unit of blood for $75 to cover my expenses.

The Methodist Hospital was affiliated with a school of nursing, and the word soon got out that three young single doctors from South Carolina had arrived. More than one nursing student came up to me in the hall and said, "Please say something southern for me."

We learned that the hospital was a very prestigious one, second only to Cedars of Lebanon, and we had some famous people as our patients. On one occasion, I was sitting in the cafeteria drinking coffee when a student nurse came in, breathless with excitement, and said, "Guess what? I just gave Roy Rogers an enema!"

Ciro's was a famous night club in Hollywood. It hosted many celebrities and was the place to see and be seen. The club's manager was a patient in the hospital and was so grateful to one of the students for the attention she had received that she invited the student to come to Ciro's. The manager waived the cover charge and told the student she was welcome to bring some friends. The student eagerly accepted the offer and invited two other students as well as Hubert, Bill, and me.

We had a good time seeing all the celebrities, most of whom I did not recognize as I had spent little time at the movies. At one point, my date and I went out on the dance floor, and she said, "Oh, look. There's Carmen Miranda. Let's dance that way, and you can bump me into her." So, I did. After that, we bumped into a number of the rich and famous.

Besides bumping into movie stars, I also did some work at the Methodist Hospital. My work at the skin cancer clinic was especially beneficial to me. I learned how to diagnose and excise many of these cancers and gained much experience.

Although I would like to have made it all the way through college and medical school without asking my family for financial assistance, my GI Bill funding finally ran out after my third year of medical school, and I had to turn to my father for help. The administration of the medical college estimated that it would cost each student a minimum of $1,800 a year to attend, including all expenses. I have always been proud of the fact that I was able to get through my last year of medical school on a personal budget of $1,200. It wasn't that my family wouldn't have given me more. It was just that I wanted to be as independent as possible, as well as being as little a burden on them as I could.

Medical School Graduate

Internship at Maumee Valley Hospital
in Toledo, Ohio

INTERNSHIP

During the final year of medical school, the big decision of where to go next was on everybody's mind. Internships, a more general training lasting one or two years, were available but there were not as many residencies, specialized training lasting for seven or more years, in 1953 as there are now. In those days, many physicians simply went into practice, sometimes with an older and more experienced physician although the trend was moving toward general, broadly based internships. Residencies in new specialties, such as obstetrics or gynecology, surgery, pediatrics, and internal medicine were also being developed. Most graduates who were going into general practice, as I was (the term "family practice" was not coined for some years), took one year of a general internship. Today's trend is toward more narrow specialization, as the wealth of material with which physicians must become familiar grows exponentially larger, making the training of generalists less and less manageable.

At the time of my graduation, the Medical College of the State of South Carolina was participating in the first national internship and residency matching program, which is a type of program that almost all medical schools use today. In such a program, a national organization sends all graduates a list of training hospitals, including information about each program. In turn, all the hospitals receive the names and credentials of the graduates. Both groups send back their choices, ranked in order of preference, and the matching organization compares and matches the preferences so that each group gets its top choices that match. The match is not binding on the students.

My first choice was Greenville General Hospital in Greenville, South Carolina, and the choice matched so I borrowed a car and took off one weekend to look it over, as I had never seen it. It seemed to be satisfactory until I asked about the amount of time I would get to spend with the hospital's indigent patients. Typically, at that time, physicians-in-training handled all indigent patients from admission to discharge with consultation when needed. However, when assigned to deal with private patients, the trainees did all the paperwork but only watched as the private physicians cared for the patients and made all the decisions. I felt that the more time I spent with patients who depended on me for the majority of their care, the better prepared I would be when the time came that I would be on my own. Unfortunately, the reply I got was that I would divide half my time with indigent patients and half with private patients. I considered the time spent on the private service wasted, so I was very disappointed. My friend Bill Miller was in the same situation and was also disappointed.

So we talked it over and both withdrew from our matching hospitals and decided to go it on our own. We found the issue of *The Journal of the American Medical Association* that identified all the internships and residencies in the country. Then we formulated our priorities. We decided to strike the teaching hospitals, because we didn't want to be involved with medical students. We wanted to consider only charity hospitals having emergency rooms and only those that had residencies in the major specialties, as we knew that most of our teaching would come from residents. We also decided not to accept less than $200 a month in salary, as we felt that we were worth at least that much. Some hospitals paid nothing, not even living expenses.

By the time we struck all the hospitals not meeting our requirements, there were only two left—Maumee Valley Hospital in Toledo, Ohio and one in Wisconsin. The only thing we knew about Wisconsin was that it was very cold, so we struck that one off the list, which left us with Maumee Valley, a 350-bed charity hospital. We called the administrator, who told us to come on.

The first time we saw Maumee Valley Hospital was the day we went there to stay—and a few months later, we found out that Wisconsin wasn't the only place where it could get very cold.

First Days at Maumee

I remember that we went to work on July 1, 1953. I was put in the emergency room—alone. As I stood there, feeling a high level of anxiety, I began to hear the sound of a siren getting closer and closer. They are coming to see me, I thought and briefly began to panic. I began to worry that I might have gone all the way through medical school and totally missed studying some condition, which, of course, my first patient would have, and I would have no idea what was wrong.

Fortunately, that did not happen.

My first busy night in the emergency room was on July fourth. There had been a big fireworks display, and that night I saw a tremendous number of patients with corneal burns. Apparently the display had gone off directly overhead, the hot ashes had drifted down and landed in people's eyes as they stared into the night sky.

Learning about Indigent Patients

Being a hospital that accepted all the indigent patients from a large city, our exposure to the poor was extensive. One of the most frequent types of patients brought to the emergency room was one who had been found lying unconscious on the street. They were the poorest of the poor and had multiple problems, including substance abuse.

I remember one such man whom I examined and admitted. It was obvious that he was intoxicated but he needed to be "worked up," as I didn't know what other problems he might have, although he had no signs of acute illness. Tuberculosis was common among these patients, but they were all debilitated from years of self-neglect. Experiences like this, during which I had so little information to go on, made me appreciate a good history from patients.

Several hours after seeing the patient, I was called to the floor, as he had lapsed into shock. I hurriedly examined him and discovered that he had perforated a peptic ulcer, an emergency requiring perforation closure and "wash out" of the stomach acids that have poured into the abdominal cavity. As I began the resuscitation process, I notified the surgeons, and the patient went straight to the operating room. He had a stormy postoperative course, and I spent a lot of time with him during the next twenty-four hours. Then he became desperately ill with pneumonia. His general physical condition had become so poor that he couldn't respond to the challenge of the infection in a normal way. These were the days before respiratory therapy teams. When his lungs filled up with fluid and pus, I had to insert a catheter into his trachea and lungs to aspirate this material to prevent him from drowning in his own fluids.

He and I had a tough ten days. He was unconscious most of that time but had brief intervals when he became lucid. I tried to treat him in a caring and nonjudgmental fashion, and he seemed to appreciate it. During his stay, however, I was transferred to another service and was no longer responsible for his care, but I went back to see him several times just to keep up with him and observe his progress.

He did at last recover and was well enough to be discharged, so I went by to see him one last time. As I looked at him, it was as if a great weight descended on me. I thought about all the work and effort he had required of me and how likely it was that when he was back on the streets, he would resume his life of self-abuse. I said to him, "Well, I guess you will just go back to drinking again."

"No, Doctor," he said. "When I opened my eyes and saw the priest giving me the last rites, I told God that if he would let me get well, I would never drink again."

As I never saw him after that, I have often hoped that he remained true to his word.

Maggots

On another occasion, a typically unconscious patient was brought in, and when I saw him, I thought, Well, here's another one. No history. So I turned his head to the right and began the physical examination by inserting the otoscope into his ear canal where I saw what appeared to be grains of white rice deep inside. This puzzled me, and I peered at them more closely. Suddenly, I realized that the grains of rice were moving and that they weren't grains of rice at all. They were maggots! When this realization hit me, I turned away and retched several times—uncontrollably.

A short time later, when I was back in control, Bill Miller came by. In the calmest and most professional manner possible, I said, "Bill, look at this ear, will you? I'm not sure what's going on." He took the otoscope and bent over the motionless patient. In a moment, he leapt back, threw himself against the wall, and began retching violently and uncontrollably.

Hospital practical jokes are not for the weak of stomach.

As for the maggots, they posed no danger to the patient. In fact, maggots do an excellent job of cleaning a wound and are easily removed by irrigating the area with hydrogen peroxide.

Psychotic Patients and Respectful Police

The respect that doctors receive from nonmedical people is often gratifying but can sometimes lead to problematic situations. One such situation occurred repeatedly in the emergency room at Maumee Valley Hospital. Many of our patients were indigent because they were mentally ill, and the police would often bring in a patient who was psychotic and unmanageable. Sometimes it would take as many as four officers to pin the patient to the examining table. Invariably, however, as soon as I walked into the examining room, all four would release the patient and spring back, as if they had suddenly been relieved of their task by the magical authority of my medical degree. They waited for the magic to take effect. It never did, of course, because the patient was caught up in a struggle with his own demons, of which I too often appeared to be one.

I remember grappling with one such patient, both of us crashing to the floor, and rolling back and forth under the partitions that separated the examining areas. I never dreamed that as a physician I would have to use the hand-to-hand combat training I had learned in the Marine Corps, but I was glad that I had learned it and that, in those days, at 6 feet 3 inches and 195 pounds, I was big and strong.

Intoxicated Patients and the Tricks of the Trade

There was a rule in the hospital that if a patient was brought in heavily intoxicated and he could not walk out without assistance, he would have to be admitted, which involved yet another history and physical and orders to be written. We tried to avoid these situations if at all possible and had developed all kinds of sobering-up treatments—some none too pleasant—to get a patient out of the hospital. After all, the reality of most such situations was that the patients were merely inebriated and would require no real medical care. Having to do a history and a physical seemed like a foolish waste of time.

I recall one man who was brought in heavily intoxicated. He could hardly speak, much less walk, but I used every trick I knew and was finally able to get him walking well enough to get him out of the emergency room. Unfortunately, no more than three minutes after he had been discharged, he was brought back in, having fallen and split his head open in the street. Not only did I have to go through the entire procedure of admitting him to the hospital, I had to suture the head wound as well.

In my admission orders, in addition to many other things, I had written to give him a mixture of dextrose and regular insulin, intravenously. This was a standard order at that time, as it was felt that this combination would hasten the metabolism of alcohol.

In about twenty minutes, though, the floor nurse called to report that this same patient had become unresponsive.

"How much insulin did you give him?" I asked.

"100 units, just as you ordered," said the nurse.

I was stunned, as that had not been my order at all.

"Give him 50 cc of 50% glucose IV," I said. "Stat. And I'll come up to check him."

I went directly to the floor, and the patient was already coming around, having received the intravenous glucose. In my order, I had written, "Give 10 u. regular insulin." The use of "u." was not an uncommon abbreviation for "unit" and continues to be used today. But the nurse had mistaken the "u" for a second zero and had given the patient 100 units of insulin—and a bout of extremely low blood sugar.

While the nurse and I were discussing this misunderstanding, the patient staggered up to the desk and said, "How do I sign my way out of this place?" He could not be dissuaded and so signed the "Leaving against Medical Advice" form and staggered off into the night.

The Beginning of My Deep Appreciation for Nurses

When not working on the day shift in the emergency room, I was assigned to one of the 30-bed inpatient wards in the hospital. Finally, there came that long-awaited day when I went up to the inpatient ward as the attending physician. I assumed a professional demeanor and introduced myself to the nurses at the nurses' desk.

"I'm glad to meet you," one of them replied. "The patient in bed 10 needs a laxative. Would you order one?"

At that point in my career I could have treated, from memory, leprosy, Tsutsuegamushi fever, and a host of other exotic diseases, but the laxative section of my brain was suddenly frozen. Here I was trying to make a good impression, and I couldn't even remember the name of a laxative!

The nurse was a kindly, middle-aged woman who, I suspect, realized my dilemma and quickly said, "One that we often use is milk of magnesia and cascara."

"That will be fine," I answered and offered a silent prayer of thanks.

This was the first of a lifetime full of experiences in which nurses proved to be valuable and caring allies.

The Pocket Knife and the Tracheostomy

One memorable day in the ward, as I was sitting at the nurses' desk, I heard the nurse call, "Doctor, please come quick!" I promptly located the nurse, hurried to her side, and was confronted with a dramatic scene.

The nurse was standing beside the bed of an elderly female patient who had both hands clutched at her throat. She was exhibiting signs of acute and total upper airway obstruction, and she couldn't breathe. I had never seen the patient before and so had no history to guide me in this dilemma.

In any event, although I didn't know why she had this problem, I knew what needed to be done. Somehow the airway had to be restored—and quickly—if she was going to have a chance to survive. If such an emergency occurred today, the nurse would probably have already brought over the crash cart so I could insert an endotracheal tube. In those days, however, endotracheal tubes were kept in central supply, about twenty minutes away. And we didn't have five minutes to spare, much less twenty.

Without hesitation, I reached into my pocket. I took out my pocketknife, which my father years ago had always required me to carry, and performed a tracheostomy, making an incision in the anterior neck and continuing into the trachea.

Having long since grown accustomed to using surgically sharp scalpels, I was surprised at how difficult it was to cut the tissue with my knife, which I obviously had not kept as sharp as my father had warned me to do. Furthermore, the patient was experiencing severe pain, as there was no time to administer any kind of anesthesia, and I had to have the nurses restrain her hands, as she was vigorously resisting my efforts to save her life. I was also acutely aware of the two carotid arteries lying on each side of my incision and of the fact that her violent movements could bring one of these into my surgical field with disastrous consequences. Finally, after what seemed a long time, but was only a few seconds, I reached the trachea and inserted the knife blade into it, making a short vertical incision.

Unfortunately, another problem immediately became obvious. Unless my knife blade was inserted into the trachea, my incision tended to close. I needed something to keep the incision open. I looked at the bedside table and saw a glass with a drinking straw in it. I took this straw and inserted it into the trachea, and that did the job, at least until I could get a regular tracheostomy tube. For the briefest of moments, I felt the satisfaction of knowing that I had adapted quickly and effectively to a critical situation. I had passed the test. Then the patient went into shock, and despite all our vigorous efforts, she died.

I never found out what the original problem was, as the family refused our requests for an autopsy. In discussions with the other physicians, the only hypothesis that seemed at all reasonable was that a major artery ruptured and compressed the trachea. Then she went slowly downhill and died from acute blood loss. The only thing that I had done was to increase her life for a few minutes and make her last moments more painful. Sometimes when you make all the right decisions for all the right reasons, the outcome is still a failure. However, such failures are the ones that you learn to accept in a medical career. It's the failures that you feel could have been avoided that eat at you.

The Contagious Disease Hospital

On the campus of the hospital was a smaller 32-bed hospital with two large wards and several private and semiprivate rooms that served as the contagious disease hospital for a wide multicounty area. The patient area in the wards was divided with partitions so we could make private rooms or multi-bed wards.

No patients ill with a contagious disease were admitted to any of the other hospitals, but were instead referred to this one. It usually had a staff of one nurse and the four interns from the larger hospital who served in rotations of one per month. Since there were usually no more than three or four patients at any one time, we simply added this rotation to our regular duties in the main hospital.

I valued such rotations, as I was able to observe and treat some of the meningitides and other unusual diseases that we did not see in the main facility. In retrospect, however, I now value my experience there not only for the clinical knowledge I gained, but for the powerful personal dramas I witnessed. This little hospital became the site of my most uplifting and devastating moments during my year in Toledo.

The Polio Epidemic

In the summer of 1953, an elderly man was brought into the hospital with a form of paralysis that was first diagnosed as being caused by a stroke. Further study led to the conclusion that he didn't have a stroke, but he was not given any other diagnosis either. As we watched over him, unable to formulate an effective treatment, his condition rapidly worsened. And within thirty-six hours, he was dead.

Other than being baffled by the man's condition and quick deterioration, none of us on the house staff placed any special significance on the case. After the autopsy, however, our thinking changed dramatically, as the pathologist brought back a diagnosis of acute poliomyelitis. We were thunderstruck. Polio at that time was a rare, deadly, and little-understood disease, but we knew that it usually appeared in epidemics, and as there was no other case of polio for several hundred miles around us, we hoped that this case had been a fluke and nothing more. We put on our best face and went about our work as usual.

Within a week, however, a 55-year-old woman came into the contagious disease hospital with the same clinical diagnosis as the old man—poliomyelitis. We were skeptical at first, but the clinical course of progressive paralysis confirmed the diagnosis. Soon after the woman appeared in the hospital, the children began to arrive and continued arriving in increasing numbers. As quickly as that, we found ourselves in the midst of a polio epidemic.

The nature of the poliovirus was such that as soon as it hit a community, virtually all the people in that community became infected. Only a very few would get the paralytic form, but the entire community, not already immune, would be infected. Once infected, whether with the non-paralytic form or the paralytic form, each person would develop immunity to the infecting organism. Epidemic diseases require a certain percentage of the population to be susceptible in order to support an epidemic, just as a wildfire requires combustible fuel. This explains why polio epidemics were widely scattered, occurring in some locations and sparing others. It also explains why the majority of the victims were children, as they would have been born after the last epidemic in their community.

Not for several years after this particular epidemic was polio's causative agent isolated and effective vaccines developed. I believe that the epidemic I experienced was part of the last large polio epidemic in this country. Today, thankfully, the Western Hemisphere is a polio-free zone, and the end is in sight for eliminating this disease from the entire world.

The contagious disease hospital was a private hospital, and each of the patients there had a private physician who usually followed the patient and prescribed the course of treatment. This time, things were a little different. Most of the private attending physicians had no experience with polio, and there was no effective treatment for the acute phase of the illness. All we could do was provide supportive care to help patients survive the acute disease, so they could go on to rehabilitation.

At that time, no one knew what caused polio or how it was spread. Furthermore, as with all deadly contagious diseases, there was an element of fear among those who treated the patients. As in the early stages of the AIDS epidemic, even dedicated physicians and nurses who dealt with polio feared for their own safety. Because of this fear, and also to reduce the risk of spreading infection, the number of people working directly with polio patients in the infectious disease hospital was reduced to the minimum.

Most attending physicians turned over total patient care to the house staff. Periodically, they would call us to check on their patients' conditions, but only rarely did they come for a visit.

Early in the epidemic, the administrator sent word to me that I was relieved of all of my other duties in the hospital and was to devote all my time to the polio patients in the infectious disease hospital—night and day. I was to be backed up by the internal medicine resident, in addition to his other duties.

So for the next six weeks I lived in that hospital—worked there, ate there, and slept there—with twenty-five to thirty acutely and gravely ill children, mostly between the ages of five and ten years. I recall that at one time, we had eight small boys who were about eight years of age who were all on respirators, critically ill and requiring almost minute-to-minute care. Fortunately, the majority of the patients did not have respiratory paralysis and were simply observed for signs of ascending paralysis until the acute disease had run its course. Then they were out of danger and could be transferred to the rehabilitation hospital for long-term therapy.

Nevertheless, I was virtually alone in charge of the situation. The medical resident was a good physician and always willing to help, but I soon knew far more than he did about caring for these patients, as I was there all the time. Sometimes I would call him to discuss a patient, and occasionally he would come over to see how we were doing, but most decisions were left to me. (He had young children at home and feared the possibility of carrying the disease to them.)

To fulfill my role, I had to learn as much as I could about ministering to these patients, as precious little was known about their care. Through my reading in the clinical literature and through my experience, I learned that there were two phases of the disease—acute and convalescent. The acute phase included a high fever and a rapidly ascending paralysis. In the convalescent phase, no fever remained, but the effects of paralysis had to be treated with various forms of rehabilitative therapy.

Forms of Therapy

I saw patients as soon as they arrived and evaluated them. They all had stiff necks and had to have a lumbar puncture to rule out meningitis, which required a radically different treatment. They were all mildly dehydrated and had to receive intravenous fluids. From there on, each patient had to have round the clock observation for if the disease progressed to bulbar poliomyelitis, in which the throat and chest muscles are paralyzed, the threat of respiratory paralysis loomed, and with that, death. In case of respiratory paralysis, the patient had to be helped to breathe through the use of a Drinker respirator, commonly known as the iron lung.

This respirator was a large, cylindrical steel barrel, closed on both ends. The bottom had a large bellows arrangement that went back and forth, effectively changing the internal air capacity of the tank by several cubic feet, twenty to thirty times a minute. There was also a large handle by which the bellows could be operated manually in case of a power failure, a dreaded event and one whose possibility hung heavily over my head all the time. The other end could be opened or closed and have an opening through which the patient's head could be protruded. This opening was sealed around the patient's neck with a tight foam collar to make it as airtight as possible. There were also ports at intervals on each side that could be opened and arms extended through a foam collar so that nursing care could be given to the patient inside. Inside was a stretcher that could slide out so the patient could be put on it, slid back into the unit, and resealed about the neck.

The unit alternately created a vacuum and a positive pressure within the chamber, and the only way for air to move between the cylinder and the atmosphere of the surrounding room was through the patient's airway. So ideally, patients breathed twenty to thirty times per minute even if their own respiratory muscles were paralyzed.

The nature of anterior poliomyelitis (anterior polio) was that it usually affected the spinal nerves, often only leading to paralysis of one or more limbs. On the other hand, bulbar poliomyelitis (bulbar polio) affected the brain stem at the junction of the brain and spinal cord. It was this type that caused problems with respiration, as this area controlled the nerves that supplied the diaphragm, which is the primary respiratory drive along with the intercostal muscles, between the ribs, and other accessory muscles of respiration.

Fortunately, the respiratory paralysis subsided fairly rapidly in these young children, and the function was recovered in most of them. Often, though, a prolonged period of rehabilitation and physical therapy was necessary. Two of the devices used during the rehabilitation period were the Rocking Bed and the Curass respirator. Both were for individuals who required a lesser degree of assistance for the laborious task of breathing with an impaired respiratory muscular system. Both devices were used to assist patients who were "addicted" to respiratory support and had to be weaned away from it. The rocking bed was simply that—a bed with a pivot in the middle that rocked up and down like a see-saw at twenty to thirty times a minute. The patients had to synchronize their breathing rhythm with the bed's rocking and assist the air exchange that occurred as the abdominal contents shifted and caused the diaphragm to move up and down.

The Curass (shield) respirator was, in a sense, a miniature of the Drinker. It consisted of two parts—a large unit that fit over the patient's chest, and a smaller unit, connected to the large unit with a large hose, which introduced positive pressure alternating with negative pressure into the large unit. Both of these units required the voluntary cooperation of the patients in the timing of the respiratory effort, as they provided only weak assistance at best.

Finally, there were Sister Kenny's hot packs. Sister Kenny was a Roman Catholic nun who, early in the effort to treat polio, developed a widely publicized treatment. It involved hot wet packs to the affected limbs in an effort to prevent paralysis. Eventually, the treatment was proven to be without value, but at the time it was one of the few treatments that we had.

In essence, the art of taking care of this disease was to determine when the patient needed to be placed in the iron lung for respiratory support. If done too early, the patients would never give in to the respirator and allow it to breathe for them, but would fight against it and attempt to breathe with their own rate and rhythm, wear themselves completely out and die. If done too late, the patient would suffer brain damage from lack of oxygen and die within a short time. So it boiled down to letting the patient go to the brink of death before stepping in with respirator support.

We also learned that a tracheostomy greatly improved the chances of survival. This opened the airway and removed the upper airway resistance to the flow of air in and out of the lungs. It also greatly simplified the management of the airway, keeping the incision area clean and free of infection, the tracheostomy tube clean and patent, etc.

Bearing the Pressure

My job really boiled down to watching the patients very closely, following them to the edge of death, and making the decision to proceed with a tracheotomy and respirator care. Very soon, all the other staff were willing for me to make all the decisions and simply did what I asked them. A call to the attending or a surgical resident usually got immediate attention and compliance with my request.

I believe that for the month during which the epidemic peaked, I treated approximately a hundred acutely ill patients and bore the weight of almost total responsibility for their care. Previously, in the other areas of Maumee Valley Hospital, my patient load had been largely adult with only a few children, and I had found that it was usually gratifying to take care of children, as they usually were sick only a day or two and responded rapidly to therapy.

Not so much in here. The children were desperately ill and often remained so for days and days. During the time that I had the eight little boys, they all lay in their respirators without moving or speaking, as all of them had tracheotomies. It's as if they had been stripped of their personalities.

How did I bear the pressure? I really don't know, except that I was totally consumed by the job, living and breathing it every day. I was probably too busy to realize the level of stress I was actually under. The one time that I took a break from the hospital occurred on an afternoon when some friends asked me to join them for a ride. The entire time I was gone, however, I worried about the situation back at the hospital. I worried that one of the respirators might have had a mechanical failure or that electric power might have shut down, which was a constant worry of mine. I recall that on one occasion, as I was writing at the desk in the nurses' station, the drinking fountain next to me cycled off. My heart leapt in panic, and I was certain that a respirator had stopped functioning. It took several minutes for my heart to stop pounding. Needless to say, my one "break" from the pressure cooker was hardly that at all, and I was relieved to get back to the little hospital and make certain everyone was all right.

I never slept an entire night. The nurses continually woke me up to ask me questions or requests that I check a patient. They were all very uneasy, as all of the patients were critically ill. Few of the nurses were accustomed to working in acute patient care and, thus, were uncomfortable with such a critical situation.

Besides the nurses on duty being uncomfortable with acute care, we were also confronted with a chronic shortage of nurses. The one staff nurse was soon overwhelmed, and the call went out over the city for nurses to volunteer for one day a week or more.

Many nurses, however, did not want to work with acute polio, not only out of fear for their own personal safety but from fear of carrying the disease home to their families.

I recall on one occasion, a physician from the local health department came out to give us a pep talk and encourage the nurses to give more of their free time to this work. He was a poor mouthpiece for such a talk, as his daily work occurred behind a desk, which brought him no closer to danger than being scalded by a hot cup of coffee. Nevertheless, he had us lined up in front of him and told us that he did not believe that the disease was at all communicable, even though the debate was swinging in that direction. He said, "There's nothing to be afraid of. You cannot catch this disease. I'm not afraid." Then he looked at me and said, "Are you afraid, doctor?"

"I'm scared to death," I answered.

And I was. We had little idea of how polio was transmitted, and many were the times that I pondered the possibility of contracting the disease. But someone had to take care of these patients, and I was a good choice, as I was not married and had no dependents. Besides, there were many other diseases that I could easily catch from my patients, none of which I wanted to catch, but that hadn't stopped me from doing my work in the past, so why should it now?

While I have never thought of myself as invincible, I do have the assurance that I am not in this life alone. God did not create me to turn me loose and then sit back to see what happens to me. He is with me and expects me to be alert for the opportunities that present themselves. I think he expects me to help those whose needs my talents seem to fit.

Of the roughly one hundred patients that came through that month, about fifteen died, about seventy went to rehabilitation, and fifteen were discharged home. We generally kept the patients until they were free of fever and showed no further advance of the paralysis. This was generally six to seven days. Then they were transferred to the rehabilitation hospital for convalescent care and rehabilitation.

The Boy with the Blocked Air Passage

Because of the tracheotomies we performed on those patients who suffered respiratory paralysis, we had to be watchful of the tracheostomy opening itself to make sure that the area of incision healed properly.

One night, a nurse called me to the bedside of an eight-year-old boy whose tracheostomy was healing and who was about ready to go to the rehabilitation hospital. There was great alarm in the nurse's voice, as the child was struggling for breath and turning blue. I saw in an instant that he had upper respiratory obstruction of a severe degree. I reasoned that the encrustation that was around the exterior of the wound probably was also around the interior and that some piece of the crust had probably broken off and been pushed by the flow of air to the vocal cords where it was lodged beneath them, causing them to close tightly in spasm (laryngeal spasm).

The nurse was frantically trying to suction the airway clear without success. The surgical resident, who had been called, appeared in the door, took one look, and ran for the operating room in the hospital to get a bronchoscope with which to look down his trachea and possibly clear the obstruction. The patient was almost black from lack of oxygen and nothing had helped. I quickly picked him up by the ankles and held him clear of the floor. Then I told the nurse, "When he coughs, slap him on the back of his chest as hard as you can." She did as I told her, and after a few moments, we were rewarded with a big cough and a chunk of almost dry mucus flying from his mouth. Immediately, the child began to breathe normally and rapidly regained his color.

A few moments later, the surgical resident raced into the room carrying a bronchoscope. He found the little boy sitting on his bed, laughing and talking.

"What happened?" he asked in surprise.

When I told him, he appeared disgruntled that he had made a useless trip. I guess he felt that he should have thought of that same solution. Several months later, after I had rotated to the emergency room, when I called him to consult on a patient, he said, "Why don't you pick him up by the legs and pound on his back?"

He did, however, come to see the patient and was in good spirits, so I assumed this remark was made in fun.

The Little Girl

One day, toward the end of the epidemic, a pretty little blond girl, about seven years old, was admitted. She was in the early stage of the disease process, and as usual, I watched her carefully. Within a few hours, I noted that her paralysis was progressing in a manner that made me uncomfortable. And by that night, I could see that if the disease continued to make the same progress, she would need to be on a respirator before morning.

I had not heard from her physician nor to my knowledge, had he visited her, so I called him and asked that he alert a surgeon, as the little girl was going to need a tracheotomy. He disagreed, saying that she hadn't looked that bad when he had seen her that morning and sent her to the hospital. He suggested that perhaps I was an alarmist. Not only did this make me angry, for I had now seen enough such cases to have no doubt about my observations, but it made me uneasy for the child, as I knew that she would have to go on a respirator, at the proper time, if she was going to live.

As time went by, the little girl got worse, her respirations became more labored and shallower. I called the physician again. Again he refused my request.

I called him the third time, and the third time he refused and said he would see her in the morning. I said, "Doctor, you had better come see her now! This patient is dying!"

Only then did he say that he would come and see for himself.

I then called the surgical resident, as we had no time to waste waiting for her physician to call a private surgeon for the tracheotomy. When the physician arrived, the surgical resident, a nurse, and I were all at the open respirator with the little girl and the surgical instruments open and ready.

A glance told the girl's doctor the whole story—she was indeed dying. He gave the order for the tracheotomy, which was done in record time; we slid her into the chamber, closed the entry about her neck, and turned on the power.

Too late. Within a short time, I pronounced her dead.

As I stepped out of the room, her parents, who had been waiting for a number of hours and who knew nothing of my conversations with their physician, came up to me and said, "Doctor, we want to thank you for all you did for her. We hate to lose her, but we know that you did your very best."

I expressed my condolences as best I could and turned away, making my way to an unoccupied storeroom where I wept uncontrollably. Tears flowed freely, and great paroxysms of grief and frustration shook my body.

When I was at last able to control myself, I stepped into the hall and tried to go about my business. The nursing staff, however, avoided my gaze, and I realized they knew and were kind enough not to interfere with my grief.

Almost fifty years later, as I write this, tears are flowing down my cheeks, and I break down in sobs from time to time. I count this as the lowest point of my career.

Some may wonder why, in these circumstances, I hadn't just taken things into my own hands and done what I knew was the right thing. There are three reasons. One is that medical school had trained me to obey orders from my superiors. Medicine works best that way, as the most skilled are usually in charge. It is a good system, even though it failed my little blond friend that day. Second, the law forbade me. The child's physician had permission to treat her. I only had permission through him. My assuming command would have been interpreted as assault, and if she had died after I had taken control illegally, I could have been charged with murder. Third, I was not too far removed from that master initiator in the discipline of obedience—the US Marine Corps. It never occurred to me to disobey orders. And yet, the very fact that I am now explaining my reasons for not doing what I knew a patient needed must indicate that I feel some measure of guilt and regret for what was not done.

A few days after the incident, I was gratified when the chief-of-staff looked me up and said, "I heard what happened, and I'm sorry. If you get in a situation like that again, call me, and I will assume control of the patient. Then you can give the correct treatment."

This was the very best thing he could have done—both for what was said and what was unsaid.

One last thought about that particular incident: I was surprised at how painful it was to cry. I had served in the marines and had believed my father when he had told me, "Men don't cry." Like most men of my generation, I had tried to live by this rule. Today, even though crying comes easier and more frequently, it almost always comes only after I have tried my best to prevent it.

The End of the Epidemic

Toward the end of the epidemic, a physician, one of the leading government authorities on infectious disease, paid us a visit. Just before he left, the entire staff was assembled, and he congratulated us on doing such a good job. Then he said, "If I ever get polio, I don't want to go to a big place like Johns Hopkins. I want to come right here and have these two"—indicating the medical resident and me—"take care of me."

After the epidemic had run its course, I visited the rehabilitation center and saw all the little patients who had passed through our small hospital. They all recognized me and shouted their greetings. When I passed the bed of one particular little boy, he called to me in a gasping voice.

"Doctor," he said, "see what I can do!"

His hand was in a splint with rubber bands that held his fingers in an extended position, straight out. As I watched, he slowly flexed one of his fingers and then extended it.

"See!" he said.

With moist eyes, I congratulated him.

Preview of Dr. Watson's
sequel
Catching the Clouds

As a boy, I thought my older brother Joe knew everything. I remember asking him all kinds of questions. And his answers to me were always the gospel.

I remember one hot summer day walking with Joe to Clouds Creek. As we strolled along the familiar dirt road to the creek, I saw—just ahead of us and moving in the same direction—the huge shadow of a cloud.

I remarked to Joe, 'If we hurry up and run and catch up to that shadow, we'll be able to walk in its shade.'

Joe just snorted. 'You can't catch a cloud,' he said.

I remember saying under my breath, 'I think I can,' as I bolted ahead, caught, and breathlessly walked in the shade of the cloud.

I never forgot that day nor the lesson that "To catch a cloud, you first have to chase it."

—From *The Cloud Chaser: A Physician's Early
Adventures* by Dr. Michael C. Watson

As he rounded that final bend into the small South Carolina town of Bamberg in July 1954, Dr. Mike Watson had no idea where his compassion, courage, sense of justice, thirst for knowledge, and sometimes stubborn, tireless perseverance were about to lead him. He did know, however, that practicing medicine in his new hometown would direct and shape his future in a way far different than farming his family's peach orchards in nearby Ridge Spring (just an hour down the road) would have.

From the moment he proved to his brother, Joe, that he could indeed catch a cloud, the younger Watson had lived his life chasing all manner of challenges. And—like that hot day on the dirt road to Clouds Creek—the newly minted M.D. was again running, this time toward the starting line to begin his professional trek (for which he had been preparing since the end of World War II) and a lifelong career as one the Palmetto State's most-celebrated physicians.

Now twenty eight years old, the returning Dr. Watson was—geographically speaking—coming full circle. Ten years earlier, he had been a wartime U.S. Marine deployed in the bloody Pacific theater.

After the war, Watson earned his undergraduate degree from Clemson College (today Clemson University), then med school at the Medical College of South Carolina in Charleston (today Medical University of South Carolina), followed by an internship in Toledo, Ohio.

But on this hot July day in the SC backcountry, it wasn't medicine or the Marines that Watson was thinking about. His focus was on whether or not he would be late for a blind date.

Dr. Herbert "Herb" Allen—who had been two years ahead in medical school and had already spent a year practicing in Bamberg—had arranged for Watson to meet (that very night) Ms. Mary Carolyn Tatum, a local daughter of a career army officer who would become the love of the young doctor's life, his wife within two years, and ultimately the mother of their six children.

Watson had no idea what was before him, professionally, in terms of stateside and overseas travel—playing a major role in the forthcoming social revolution of the 1950s, '60s, '70s, and '80s, and literally making SC history. His life's journey was about to take him to places he had never heard of and ideas he could not then have imagined: mission trips (as a Methodist church leader) in developing countries; direct involvement in the conflict of race relations in the Jim Crow South—incurring the wrath of the federal government as he stood as a strong advocate for public-school desegregation—comforting the poor as a county health officer, creating the Dawn Center, a long-term treatment for alcoholism, and essentially evolving into the man who would be known as the lowcountry's "AIDS doctor"; disputatiously winning that distinction by choosing to treat AIDS patients at a time that most would not. And taking his courage and compassion several steps beyond his practice—again, chasing the elusive shadow of the cloud—leading an effort to dismantle a local drug den by turning it into an after-school program. All this, as he daily saved lives, tended the sick and injured (often for little or no fee or perhaps for a basketful of vegetables), comforted families, and delivered untold numbers of newborns, including baby Nikki Haley, the future Governor of South Carolina.

The six-decade journey on which Dr. Watson was about to embark would provide him with many clouds to chase, problems to solve, and needs to comfort. His life would be filled with purpose.

He is grateful for this chance to share his story.

Bamberg's Main Street in the 1950s

How I Picked Bamberg:
A Place to Put My
Arms Around

In April of 1954, I was finishing my internship at Maumee Valley Hospital and had no hint as to where I could go into practice. For quite a while, I had been considering the possibility of becoming a medical missionary. From the time I was a child and knew of my mother's work with Methodist missions, this possibility had always been before me. Certainly my work with the poor of Charleston and Toledo had inclined me in that direction. Further, the stories of brave missionaries working in far, exotic places had long been popularized in books and film. For my generation, in particular, missionary work in China held a special attraction. But China had recently come under the rule of Mao Zedong, and the Communists were actively driving missionaries out of the country, which seemed to close off the most appealing opportunity for missionary work. Furthermore, I was concerned about my parents. They were getting on in age and had no children left in Ridge Spring. As my sisters, Elizabeth and Pat, and my older brother Joe had all moved away—though Joe would later return—I felt that I must put off serious thoughts of immediate missionary involvement until I had some idea about their safekeeping and future.

Finally, there was the very practical and immediate need to earn a living and pay off the loan on the car that I had just

bought. I expressed my concerns at the hospital, and the administrator very grudgingly gave me several days off to come to South
Carolina and look around. (In those days, vacation time was not
in the contract for interns.) I drove home, and as I did, I decided
I should try to find a practice within fifty miles of Ridge Spring
so I wouldn't be far away from my parents. Other than that, my
plans were open to whatever opportunities came my way.

The first morning after arriving home when I came downstairs to breakfast, my father remarked that there was a notice in
the paper of the death of Dr. Malcolm Stuckey of Bamberg, and
this might be a good place to inquire. I had already decided that
my first stop would be the Medical College in Charleston, but
Bamberg was right on the way, so I decided to stop there on my
way to Charleston.

Bamberg was a town of about 3,800 people set in the tall
pines and sandy soil of South Carolina's coastal plain, about an
hour and a half inland from Charleston. It was chartered in 1855
and became the seat of Bamberg County in 1897. When I first
arrived, Bamberg was a small, bustling town centered on the
intersection of Highways 78 and 301 and the old Charleston-
Hamburg railroad. Like many Southern towns, Bamberg had
grown up along the railroad, which was used to transport the
county's cotton and timber products to distant markets. Today,
the railroad has ceased operating, and its level, paved bed is now
used as a biking and jogging path. In 1954, however, the railroad was still a viable part of a growing community. When I first
set foot in town, Bamberg had recently renovated and moved its
courthouse and, more importantly to me, built a thirty-two-bed
hospital (Bamberg County Memorial Hospital).

When I pulled onto the main road of shops in the spring of
1954, I noticed several pharmacies in operation. Back then, many
small-town doctors maintained makeshift offices in the back of
drugstores, and I knew that pharmacists were among the best
sources of information about the goings-on in town. I pulled

over at the sign for Mac's Drugstore and went in and introduced myself to Alex McCrackin, a pharmacist and part owner of the place. After a few cordialities, I asked if Bamberg was in need of a doctor. Mr. McCrackin's reply was noncommittal, but he was not discouraging. As I had an appointment with the dean of the medical school that same day—to ask him about any openings for establishing a practice that he may have heard about—I decided to bear Bamberg in mind and come back another time.

Continuing the Search

In Charleston, the dean was polite but firm in his opinion, and my visit with him was very short. He said, "You see that file cabinet? It is full of letters from places that have asked me to recommend them to a physician looking for a place to practice. I am not going to show you any of them. Instead, I am going to tell you to go find a place where you would like to live and move there and set up an office. Your practice will take care of itself."

I reflected on this advice while driving home and concluded it was sound. Even then, when I was still unsettled about what my plans for the future should be, I guess I was looking for a place where I would feel comfortable living and could commit myself to the community.

Word traveled fast about my availability (many towns were in need of doctors in the early 1950s), and I began to get telephone calls from around the state. Most were from more than fifty miles from Ridge Spring and easy to turn down. Bamberg remained one of my top choices, although at this point my first preference was Abbeville. It was an old historic town, and several of the young couples there had gone out of their way to make me feel welcome. Abbeville had an older physician and a younger one who had been practicing there for about two years. I asked the younger physician first about his practice and the local hospital, and all his answers were satisfactory. Then I asked him about the town as a place to live.

"I wouldn't know," he replied. "In the two years I've been here, I've been too busy to learn about the community."

This answer turned me around in a hurry. It wasn't that I minded hard work. In fact, it was just the opposite. I knew myself well enough to assume that I probably wouldn't turn down any person in need and so would end up putting in at least as many hours as the young doctor with whom I was talking. And if that were the case, how would I ever find time for a social life or the opportunity to meet the future Mrs. Watson?

This question reflected how uncertain I was about what I ought to do with my life and skills. I had always wanted a family—I can recognize some of myself in my son Cal, who also has a strong urge toward family life—and I knew I'd be comfortable in a small country town. It's the world that I had grown up in. Besides, there was much poverty in rural South Carolina at the time (as there continues to be) and a great need for physicians, so I knew I could do good work there.

But I also continued to think that God might want me to be a medical missionary. After all, I was big and strong, and I had always shown the ability to keep going when things got tough. Those were qualities that would come in handy if I were called to missionary work.

So I returned to Bamberg still much in doubt about my intentions. In Bamberg I met with Dr. Herbert "Herb" Allen, who had been two years ahead of me in medical school and had spent a little more than a year practicing in Bamberg. He encouraged me to come and told me I would be welcome to the job of giving all anesthesia at the hospital. He said that he was getting too busy for this and wanted to give it up and devote all his time to his general practice. There was another young physician in town, Sam Rankin, but he didn't plan on staying. He had been a medical missionary in China and planned to return to the mission field as soon as possible, perhaps within a year. This, of course, meant that there would be less competition for me, but it also reminded me that I was still considering a missionary role myself.

Nevertheless, I liked the feeling of Bamberg and appreciated the warm reception I had received there. It was a smaller town than Abbeville, and I was more likely to find time for a social life.

H. J. Stuckey and Settling on Bamberg

And then there was Dr. H. J. Stuckey (no relation, as it turned out, to the deceased Dr. Malcolm Stuckey).

As I was leaving the front of the hospital after my meeting with Herb Allen, Dr. Stuckey met me at the door. I found out later that he was insatiably curious and had heard about my visit with Alex McCrackin and had hoped to meet me if I returned. In a matter of moments, he found out, in great detail, who I was, where I was from, information about my parents, and what families I was related to. In the rural South at the time (and still to some extent), it was always of great importance to determine whether or not someone came from a "good" family. My answers must have been satisfactory, for he seemed delighted at the possibility that I might settle in Bamberg.

When we got around to the question of setting up a practice, he said, "Oh yes, you'll have a good life here and maybe earn $9,000 a year if you make some good investments."

It sounded like a princely sum at the time, or at least a solid upper-middle class income. So being encouraged by the people I had met and having the feeling that this might be the sort of town I could wrap my arms around, I determined to begin my medical career in Bamberg, South Carolina.

As for missionary work, I decided to leave that decision to God. Because of the tremendous demands of such work, I decided that a medical missionary should not marry and should be dedicated to one thing. I believed that it would be unfair of me to require a wife to make the sort of sacrifices that a mission-ary's wife would have to make. Plus, I felt that the single-minded devotion that God would require of me as a missionary would, of necessity, make me questionable husband material. Therefore, I decided that if God sent me a wife, that would be his sign to me that he wanted me to stay in Bamberg.

Return to Toledo to Finish Internship

Having chosen the place where I would begin my career, I went back to Maumee Valley Hospital—from shirtsleeves in Bamberg to a snowstorm in Toledo. Before returning to Toledo, though, I stopped in Ridge Spring and told Father and Mama about my decision to practice in Bamberg. They seemed pleased with that decision, and I didn't mention my ponderings about the mission field—not to them nor anyone else.

Back in Toledo, I took a one-month course at the McKesson School of Anesthesia, as I felt that I did not know enough about the administration of anesthesia to take over that function at Bamberg County Hospital. I was also very aware that I would soon be on my own, and I was determined to make my experience in Toledo as profitable as possible. Therefore, as the anesthesia school met only in the mornings, I decided to work in pathology in the afternoons and performed all the autopsies done in the hospital. Autopsy is the master teacher and always has been. You see all the very sickest patients in the hospital and can read their history and unravel the disease process. I was determined to learn as much as I could during my year in Toledo.

Setting Up Practice

When I finally moved to Bamberg in July of 1954, Herb Allen arranged for me to room in the home of the county sheriff, John Byrd Zeigler, and his wife, Gene. I ate my meals at Ziggy's, a local restaurant, and there I got to know Harold Bair, a young single man who was an accountant and the treasurer of the Bamberg Textile Mill. Eventually my irregular hours as a physician created a minor problem for the Zeiglers, so Harold and I rented an apartment together.

Herb Allen also found a practical nurse who agreed to assist me, and Dr. Malcolm Stuckey's widow agreed to rent his office to me so I would have a place to start. I then contacted a surgical supply house and arranged to buy equipment on an extended payment period. Between my ordinary living expenses and my payments on my car, I had not been able to save very much of my $200 monthly salary. My father went to the bank and negotiated and co-signed a loan of $1,000 for me.

At last I was about to start on the career for which I had trained so long.

Continue to read Dr. Watson's gripping and entertaining stories in *Catching the Clouds, A Physician's Purpose Filled Life.*

ACKNOWLEDGEMENTS

Creating *The Cloud Chaser* and *Catching the Clouds* has been a labor of love for 15 years. I have always enjoyed storytelling, but the journey into writing started with my children's request and a few stories written as a Christmas gift for them in 1997. Over the years, others requested that I document the creation of the missions program in the United Methodist Church so combining both efforts made sense. As the stories developed, I realized that my life, like most, reflects cultural changes over the decades that may interest a broader audience.

There are so many to thank for the end result. The family pictures, many of which I took, were dug out and sorted primarily by Mary Carolyn - no small feat. Mary Carolyn has been my cheerleader on the book and in life. She and Barbara Loadholt Mirmow, her college friend, both spent time proofing as my memories were cranked out. Caroline, the books' editor and my daughter, has always been a big proponent of getting my story down on paper, finding resources, proofing, and figuring out things like cover design and photo layout. My son, Cal, the family historian, had a full repertoire of pictures and, like Mary Carolyn, many facts to support the family stories. Discussions with all my children and my siblings prompted many memories.

I cannot thank my office staff enough for their kindness and professionalism over the years. Both before and after I retired, Laura Hoffman provided hours of administrative support and is still a constant source of information and help. Alice Fleming,

Director of the Mission Cottage, supplied photographs of children taking part in the program.

Initially Ken Huggins and later Steve Hoffius spent much time helping organize and edit a massive amount of material. Caroline has been part of my team from the beginning and handled all editing and publisher-related efforts over the last several years. W. Thomas Smith Jr. had a hand in polishing the Preface for *The Cloud Chaser* and has given advice along the way.

Almost all of the generous people who supported my life's work have provided encouragement at times when I needed it most. Dr. Hal Crosswell and Rev. George Strait, who played such critical roles in the success of our missions program, provided pictures and filled in blanks. Rev. Nick Elliott provided support on the local and jurisdictional levels. Doris Chambers and Lee McMillan, both excellent administrative assistants with the United Methodist Church and SC United Methodist Volunteers in Missions, readily provided help whenever asked.

Dr. and Mrs. Ajit Randhawa have generously supported this effort by providing information and photographs. Their daughter, Nikki Haley, Governor of South Carolina, graciously included words of support in her own book, *Can't is Not an Option,* as well as her inspirational endorsement of *Catching the Clouds.* Dr. H. Biemann Othersen, a former classmate and current professor with the College of Medicine at MUSC, was kind enough to provide promotional assistance for *The Cloud Chaser.* Dr. Henry Tisdale, President of Claflin University, Mel Williams and other staff members generously provided pictures and requested information.

In short, these books have been a journey of love, commitment, and devotion. Because I have received so much from so many, it is overwhelming to try to include names of everyone that contributed to this effort. For those named here - and those that I will remember later that should have been included - thank you for your generous support and guidance. I am forever in your debt.